DC Moore

The Empire

Methuen Drama

Published by Methuen Drama 2010

1 3 5 7 9 10 8 6 4 2

Methuen Drama
A & C Black Publishers Limited
36 Soho Square
London W1D 3QY
www.methuendrama.com

ISBN: 978 1 408 13056 8

A CIP catalogue record for this book
is available from the British Library

Typeset by Country Setting, Kingsdown, Kent
Printed and bound in Great Britain by
CPI Cox & Wyman Ltd, Reading, Berkshire

Caution

ROYAL COURT

DRUM THEATRE

PLYMOUTH THEATRES

Royal Court Theatre and Drum Theatre Plymouth
present

THE EMPIRE

by **DC Moore**

First performance at the Royal Court Jerwood Theatre Upstairs,
Sloane Square, London, on 31 March 2010.

First performance at the Drum Theatre Plymouth on 13 May 2010.

First performance at Elephant and Castle Shopping Centre
as part of the Royal Court's Theatre Local season on 2 June 2010.

JERWOOD
NEW PLAYWRIGHTS

Supported by the Jerwood Charitable Foundation

THE EMPIRE
by **D C Moore**

Cast
in order of appearance

Gary **Joe Armstrong**
Hafizullah **Josef Altin**
Zia **Nav Sidhu**
Jalandar **Imran Khan**
Simon **Rufus Wright**

Director **Mike Bradwell**
Designer **Bob Bailey**
Lighting Designer **Jason Taylor**
Sound Designer **Nick Manning**
Casting Director **Amy Ball**
Assistant Director **Jane Fallowfield**
Production Manager **Tariq Rifaat**
Fight Director **Malcolm Ranson**
Stage Managers **Anna-Maria Casson, Naomi Foster**
Costume Supervisor **Iona Kenrick**
Stage Management Work Placement **Genna Hill**
Set built and painted by **TR2, Theatre Royal Plymouth
  Production Centre**

The Royal Court and Stage Management wish to thank
the following for their help with this production:

**Captain Alexander Forster, Captain Jason Glyn-Roche,
Corporal of Horse Steve Wyard, Patrick Hennessy, Talal Majab,
Lila Allen, Canonbury Healthcare and Saka Water.**

DC MOORE (WRITER)

FOR THE ROYAL COURT: DC Moore's first play, Alaska, opened at the Royal Court Theatre Upstairs in 2007.

DC Moore is currently writing his third full-length play, Town, for the Royal & Derngate, Northampton. The Royal & Derngate also recently produced his monologue, Honest, which was performed at The Mailcoach pub, Northampton in March 2010.

AWARDS: Awarded the inaugural Tom Erhardt Award for promising new playwrights for Alaska (Royal Court Theatre).

The Empire is DC Moore's second full-length play.

JOSEF ALTIN (HAFIZULLAH)

FOR THE ROYAL COURT: Credible Witness.

OTHER THEATRE INCLUDES: Mrs Affleck (National Theatre); Kingfisher Blue (Bush); Low Dat (Birmingham Rep); Mind The Gap (Y Touring); Badnuff (Soho).

TELEVISION INCLUDES: Law and Order II, Misfits, Beautiful People II, Being Human, The Bill, MI High, New Tricks, Ten Days to War, God On Trial, West 10 LDN, Little Miss Jocelyn, No Heroics, Omid, Pulling, Robin Hood, Soundproof, Peep Show, Happy Slapz, The Golden Hour, Murphy's Law, Blackpool.

FILM INCLUDES: Eastern Promises, Poppy Shakespeare, The Young Victoria, Boy A, Ruby Blue, Sixty 6, Gypo, Stoned, Dirty Pretty Things.

JOE ARMSTRONG (GARY)

THEATRE INCLUDES: Orphans (Traverse/Soho); A Night at the Dogs, Protection (Soho); How Love is Spelt (Bush).

TELEVISION INCLUDES: Breaking the Mould, Whistleblowers, The Last Detective, Party Animals, Robin Hood, Inspector Lynley, Coming Up, Rose & Maloney, Midsomer Murders, Foyle's War, Blackpool, Waking the Dead, Passer By, Between the Sheets, The Bill.

FILM INCLUDES: A Passionate Woman, A Ticket Too Far.

BOB BAILEY (DESIGNER)

FOR THE ROYAL COURT: The Lying Kind.

OTHER THEATRE INCLUDES: Bottle Universe, The God Botherers, Stitching, Trance, Pumpgirl (Bush); Hijra (Bush/Plymouth); Love Me Tonight (Hampstead); Angels In America, Charley's Aunt (Crucible); Paradise Bound, The Way Home (Liverpool Everyman); The New Statesman (Trafalgar Studios/tour); Side by Side by Sondheim (The Venue, Leicester Square); Lieutenant of Inishmore, The Real Thing, Anything Goes, (UK tours); Never Forget (Savoy/tours); Rent, Hair, Cabaret, An Ideal Husband (English Theatre, Frankfurt); Translations, Moll Flanders (Bristol Old Vic); Edward Gant's Amazing Feats of Loneliness (Drum, Plymouth).

OPERA AND DANCE INCLUDE: All Nighter, Horse-Play (Royal Ballet); Tosca (Nationale Reisopera, Netherlands); Don Giovanni (British Youth Opera); Fedora, Macbeth, La Sonnambula, Manon Lescaut (Opera Holland Park); Falstaff (Guildhall Opera); About Face (ROH2).

AWARDS: 1999 Time Out Designer of The Year (set only) DV8's The Happiest Day Of My Life (UK/European Tour).

MIKE BRADWELL (DIRECTOR)

FOR THE ROYAL COURT: An Honorable Trade, Susan's Breast's, A Bed of Roses, Doing the Business.

OTHER THEATRE INCLUDES: Mrs Gauguin & Mrs Vershinin (Almeida/ Riverside & Kampnagel, Hamburg); Tuesday's Child (Stratford East); The Cockroach Trilogy (National & International tour); The Dalkey Archive (Long Wharf Theatre). Various productions at The Tricycle Theatre, West Yorkshire Playhouse, King's Head Theatre, Hampstead Theatre, The Science Fiction Theatre Of Liverpool, The National Theatre Of Brent.

FOR THE BUSH THEATRE (As Artistic Director 1996 -2007): Love And Understanding, Dogs Barking, Dead Sheep, Shang-a-Lang, Little Baby Nothing, Howie The Rookie, Normal, Flamingos, Blackbird, Resident Alien, Airsick, When You Cure Me, adrenalin…heart, The Glee Club, The Girl With Red Hair, Crooked, Pumpgirl.

WRITING CREDITS INCLUDE: The Writing On The Wall, Games Without Frontiers, Chains Of Love, Happy Feet, I Am A Donut.

Mike was Associate Director at The Royal Court Theatre from 1984-1986.

Mike founded Hull Truck Theatre Company in 1971. He wrote and directed all of their shows for ten years.

JANE FALLOWFIELD (ASSISTANT DIRECTOR)

THEATRE INCLUDES: Traces (Paines Plough); Dunsinane (RSC).

Jane is Senior Reader at Paines Plough and script reader for the National Theatre, the BBC writersroom and ATC.

Jane co-runs Root Theatre.

IMRAN KHAN (JALANDER)

TELEVISION INCLUDES: Strike Back, Political Crime: The Murder of Naji Ali, Terror In the Sky.

FILM INCLUDES: Sand Serpents, Guns.

RADIO INCLUDES: English in Afghanistan & Silverstreet, BBC.

NICK MANNING (SOUND DESIGNER)

THEATRE INCLUDES: Ghost Stories, Three Sisters, Jack and the Beanstalk, Comedians, The Jitterbug Blitz, Hang On, Cinderella, Spyski!, Depth Charge, Love – the Musical, The Birthday Party, The Resistible Rise of Arturo Ui, Beauty and the Beast, Accidental Heroes, Absolute Beginners, Ramayana, Metamorphosis, Too Close to Home, The Odyssey, Some Girls Are Bigger Than Others, The Firework-Maker's Daughter, Don Juan, Oliver Twist, Pericles, Camille, A Christmas Carol, The Prince of Homburg, Aladdin, The Servant and Pinocchio (Lyric Hammersmith); Gizmo Love, Excuses, Out of Our Heads (ATC); The Unsinkable Clerk (Network of Stuff); Grumpy Old Women 2, Britt on Britt, Grumpy Old Women (Avalon); Airsick, Crooked, When You Cure Me (Bush); Darwin in Malibu (Hampstead); The Master and Margarita (National Youth Theatre); Rabbit (Frantic Assembly); Great Expectations (Bristol Old Vic).

Nick is Head of Sound at the Lyric Hammersmith.

NAV SIDHU (ZIA)

THEATRE INCLUDES: Arabian Nights (RSC).

TELEVISION INCLUDES: Spooks.

JASON TAYLOR (LIGHTING DESIGNER)

THEATRE INCLUDES: Six Degrees Of Separation, National Anthems (Old Vic); Duet for One (Almeida/Vaudeville Theatre); Rum and Coca Cola (ETT tour); Awaking Beauty (Scarborough); Rainman (Apollo Theatre); Flashdance, Blackbird, How The Other Half Loves, Lady In The Van, Single Spies, Pirates of Penzance (National tour); Year of the Rat (West Yorks Playhouse); Pygmalion (Broadway); Peter Hall Season (Bath); Journeys End (Broadway); Absurd Person Singular (Garrick Theatre); The Letter, Honour (Wyndhams Theatre); Entertaining Angels (Chichester /national tour); BCC (National Theatre); What the Butler Saw (Criterion); Glorious (Duchess/ Birmingham Rep); The God Of Hell (Donmar); Some Girls(s) (Gielgud); Twelfth Night (Albery Theatre); Journeys End (Comedy/Duke of Yorks/National Tour); High Society (Shaftesbury); Madness Of George 3rd (West Yorkshire Playhouse); Us and Them, The Dead Eye Boy (Hampstead Theatre); Abigails Party (New Ambassadors/Whitehall/National tour); Pretending To Be Me (Comedy Theatre); Little Shop Of Horrors (West Yorkshire Playhouse); The Cleaning (Shared Experience); Office (Edinburgh International Festival); Iolanthe, The Mikado and Yeoman of The Guard (Savoy Theatre); 20 seasons (Open Air Theatre London); Kindertransport (Vaudeville Theatre); Rosencrantz and Guildenstern (Piccadilly Theatre); And then there were none (Duke Of York's Theatre); Great Balls of Fire (Cambridge Theatre).

Jason has also designed at a number of regional theatres.

RUFUS WRIGHT (SIMON)

THEATRE INCLUDES: Serious Money (Birmingham Rep); Private Lives (Hampstead); Crown Matrimonial (UK Tour); Frost/Nixon, Mary Stuart (Donmar/West End); Journey's End (West End); Hay Fever (Basingstoke Haymarket); The Madness of George III (West Yorkshire Playhouse/Birmingham Rep); Trust Byron (Gate/UK Tour); Life with an Idiot, Franziska (Gate); Single Spies (West Yorkshire Playhouse); The Secret Garden (Salisbury Playhouse); The Backroom (Soho); The Last Sortie (King's Head); Richard II (Pleasance); The Tempest (Brave New World).

TELEVISION INCLUDES: Daughters, The Thick of It, Taking the Flak, The Bill, Fanny Hill: Memoirs of a Woman of Pleasure, Doctors, Extras, Quatermass Experiment, P.O.W, The Secret, Bomber, Boyz Unlimited, Medea Masterclass.

FILM INCLUDES: Swinging with the Finkels, The Special Relationship, Jean Charles, Quantum of Solace, Spy Game.

RADIO INCLUDES: The Devil Was Here Yesterday, I'm Still the Same Paul, Fabulous, The Caspar Logue Affair, A Dish of Pomegranates, Nyama, Lennon, A Week In The Life, The Believers, North by Northamptonshire, Shakespeare's Vortigern and Rowena.

JERWOOD
NEW PLAYWRIGHTS

Since 1994 Jerwood New Playwrights has contributed to 66 new plays at the Royal Court including Joe Penhall's SOME VOICES, Mark Ravenhill's SHOPPING AND FUCKING (co-production with Out of Joint), Ayub Khan Din's EAST IS EAST (co-production with Tamasha), Martin McDonagh's THE BEAUTY QUEEN OF LEENANE (co-production with Druid Theatre Company), Conor McPherson's THE WEIR, Nick Grosso's REAL CLASSY AFFAIR, Sarah Kane's 4.48 PSYCHOSIS, Gary Mitchell's THE FORCE OF CHANGE, David Eldridge's UNDER THE BLUE SKY, David Harrower's PRESENCE, Simon Stephens' HERONS, Roy Williams' CLUBLAND, Leo Butler's REDUNDANT, Michael Wynne's THE PEOPLE ARE FRIENDLY, David Greig's OUTLYING ISLANDS, Zinnie Harris' NIGHTINGALE AND CHASE, Grae Cleugh's FUCKING GAMES, Rona Munro's IRON, Richard Bean's UNDER THE WHALEBACK, Ché Walker's FLESH WOUND, Roy Williams' FALLOUT, Mick Mahoney's FOOD CHAIN, Ayub Khan Din's NOTES ON FALLING LEAVES, Leo Butler's LUCKY DOG, Simon Stephens' COUNTRY MUSIC, Laura Wade's BREATHING CORPSES, Debbie Tucker Green's STONING MARY, David Eldridge's INCOMPLETE AND RANDOM ACTS OF KINDNESS, Gregory Burke's ON TOUR, Stella Feehily's O GO MY MAN, Simon Stephens' MOTORTOWN, Simon Farquhar's RAINBOWKISS, April de Angelis, Stella Feehily, Tanika Gupta, Chloe Moss and Laura Wade's CATCH, Mike Bartlett's MY CHILD, Polly Stenham's THAT FACE, Alexi Kaye Campbell's THE PRIDE, Fiona Evans' SCARBOROUGH, Levi David Addai's OXFORD STREET and Bola Agbaje's GONE TOO FAR!

Last year Jerwood New Playwrights supported Alia Bano's SHADES, Polly Stenham's TUSK TUSK and Tim Crouch's THE AUTHOR. So far in 2010, Jerwood New Playwrights has supported Bola Agbaje's OFF THE ENDZ. Jerwood New Playwrights is supported by the Jerwood Charitable Foundation.

The Jerwood Charitable Foundation is dedicated to imaginative and responsible revenue funding of the arts, supporting emerging artists to develop and grow at important stages in their careers and across all art forms.

www.jerwoodcharitablefoundation.org

Polly Stenham's TUSK TUSK
(photo: Johan Persson)

Alia Bano's SHADES
(photo: Manuel Harlan)

THE ENGLISH STAGE COMPANY
AT THE ROYAL COURT THEATRE

'For me the theatre is really a religion or way of life. You must decide what you feel the world is about and what you want to say about it, so that everything in the theatre you work in is saying the same thing ... A theatre must have a recognisable attitude. It will have one, whether you like it or not.'

George Devine, first artistic director of the English Stage Company: notes for an unwritten book.

photo: Stephen Cummiskey

As Britain's leading national company dedicated to new work, the Royal Court Theatre produces new plays of the highest quality, working with writers from all backgrounds, and addressing the problems and possibilities of our time.

"The Royal Court has been at the centre of British cultural life for the past 50 years, an engine room for new writing and constantly transforming the theatrical culture." Stephen Daldry

Since its foundation in 1956, the Royal Court has presented premieres by almost every leading contemporary British playwright, from John Osborne's Look Back in Anger to Caryl Churchill's A Number and Tom Stoppard's Rock 'n' Roll. Just some of the other writers to have chosen the Royal Court to premiere their work include Edward Albee, John Arden, Richard Bean, Samuel Beckett, Edward Bond, Leo Butler, Jez Butterworth, Martin Crimp, Ariel Dorfman, Stella Feehily, Christopher Hampton, David Hare, Eugène Ionesco, Ann Jellicoe, Terry Johnson, Sarah Kane, David Mamet, Martin McDonagh, Conor McPherson, Joe Penhall, Lucy Prebble, Mark Ravenhill, Simon Stephens, Wole Soyinka, Polly Stenham, David Storey, Debbie Tucker Green, Arnold Wesker and Roy Williams.

"It is risky to miss a production there." Financial Times

In addition to its full-scale productions, the Royal Court also facilitates international work at a grass roots level, developing exchanges which bring young writers to Britain and sending British writers, actors and directors to work with artists around the world. The research and play development arm of the Royal Court Theatre, The Studio, finds the most exciting and diverse range of new voices in the UK. The Studio runs play-writing groups including the Young Writers Programme, Critical Mass for black, Asian and minority ethnic writers and the biennial Young Writers Festival. For further information, go to www.royalcourttheatre.com/ywp.

"Yes, the Royal Court is on a roll. Yes, Dominic Cooke has just the genius and kick that this venue needs... It's fist-bitingly exciting." Independent

Supported by
**ARTS COUNCIL
ENGLAND**

PROGRAMME SUPPORTERS

The Royal Court (English Stage Company Ltd) receives its principal funding from Arts Council England, London. It is also supported financially by a wide range of private companies, charitable and public bodies, and earns the remainder of its income from the box office and its own trading activities.

The Genesis Foundation supports the Royal Court's work with International Playwrights. The Jerwood Charitable Foundation supports new plays by new playwrights through the Jerwood New Playwrights series. Theatre Local is sponsored by Bloomberg.

The Artistic Director's Chair is supported by a lead grant from The Peter Jay Sharp Foundation, contributing to the activities of the Artistic Director's office. Over the past ten years the BBC has supported the Gerald Chapman Fund for directors.

ROYAL COURT DEVELOPMENT ADVOCATES
John Ayton
Elizabeth Bandeen
Tim Blythe
Anthony Burton
Sindy Caplan
Sarah Chappatte
Cas Donald (Vice Chair)
Allie Esiri
Celeste Fenichel
Anoushka Healy
Stephen Marquardt
Emma Marsh (Chair)
Mark Robinson
William Russell
Deborah Shaw Marquardt (Vice Chair)
Nick Wheeler
Daniel Winterfeldt

PUBLIC FUNDING
Arts Council England, London
British Council

CHARITABLE DONATIONS
American Friends of the Royal Court Theatre
Anthony Burton
Gerald Chapman Fund
Columbia Foundation
Credit Suisse First Boston Foundation*
Cowley Charitable Trust
The Edmond de Rothschild Foundation*
Do Well Foundation Ltd*
The D'Oyly Carte Charitable Trust
Frederick Loewe Foundation*
Genesis Foundation
The Goldsmiths' Company
The H and G de Freitas Charitable Trust
Jerwood Charitable Foundation
John Thaw Foundation
John Lyon's Charity
The Laura Pels Foundation*
Marina Kleinwort Trust
The Martin Bowley Charitable Trust
The Andrew W. Mellon Foundation
The Patchwork Charitable Foundation*
Paul Hamlyn Foundation

Jerome Robbins Foundation*
Rose Foundation
Royal College of Psychiatrists
The Peter Jay Sharp Foundation*
Sobell Foundation

CORPORATE SUPPORTERS & SPONSORS
BBC
Bloomberg
Coutts & Co
Ecosse Films
Gymbox
Moët & Chandon

BUSINESS BENEFACTORS & MEMBERS
Grey London
Hugo Boss
Lazard
Bank of America Merrill Lynch
Vanity Fair

AMERICAN FRIENDS OF THE ROYAL COURT
Rachel Bail
Francis Finlay
Amanda Foreman & Jonathan Barton
Imelda Liddiard
Stephen McGruder & Angeline Goreau
Alexandra Munroe & Robert Rosenkranz
Ben Rauch & Margaret Scott
David & Andrea Thurm
Amanda Vaill & Tom Stewart
Monica Voldstad
Franklin Wallis

INDIVIDUAL MEMBERS

ICE-BREAKERS
Act IV
Anonymous
Rosemary Alexander
Ossi & Paul Burger
Mrs Helena Butler
Lindsey Carlon
Virginia Finegold
Charlotte & Nick Fraser
David Lanch
Collette & Peter Levy
Watcyn Lewis
Mr & Mrs Peter Lord
David Marks QC
Nicola McFarland

Janet & Michael Orr
Pauline Pinder
Mr & Mrs William Poeton
The Really Useful Group
Lois Sieff OBE
Gail Steele
Nick & Louise Steidl

GROUND-BREAKERS
Anonymous
Moira Andreae
Jane Attias*
Elizabeth & Adam Bandeen
Dr Kate Best
Philip Blackwell
Stan & Val Bond
Mrs D H Brett
Sindy & Jonathan Caplan
Mr & Mrs Gavin Casey
Tim & Caroline Clark
Kay Ellen Consolver
Clyde Cooper
Ian Cormack
Mrs D H Brett
Sindy & Jonathan Caplan
Mr & Mrs Gavin Casey
Tim & Caroline Clark
Kay Ellen Consolver
Clyde Cooper
Ian Cormack
Allie Esiri
Celeste & Peter Fenichel
Margy Fenwick
The Edwin Fox Foundation
John Garfield
Beverley Gee
Lydia & Manfred Gorvy
Nick & Julie Gould
Lord & Lady Grabiner
Richard & Marcia Grand*
Nick Gray
Reade & Elizabeth Griffith
Don & Sue Guiney
Uill Hackel and Andrzej Zarzyeli
Douglas & Mary Hampson
The David Hyman Charitable Trust
Nicholas Josefowitz
David P Kaskel & Christopher A Teano
Peter & Maria Kellner*
Steve Kingshott
Mrs Joan Kingsley & Mr Philip Kingsley
Mr & Mrs Pawel Kisielewski
Kathryn Ludlow
Emma Marsh
David & Elizabeth Miles

Barbara Minto
North Street Trust
Murray North
Gavin & Ann Neath
William Plapinger & Cassie Murray*
Wendy Press
Serena Prest
Mr & Mrs Tim Reid
Mark Robinson
Paul & Gill Robinson
Paul & Jill Ruddock
William & Hilary Russell
Sally & Anthony Salz
Jenny Sheridan
The Melanie & Michael Sherwood Foundation
Anthony Simpson & Susan Boster
Sheila Steinberg
Brian D. Smith
Samantha & Darren Smith
Carl & Martha Tack
The Ury Trust
Edgar & Judith Wallner
Nick & Chrissie Wheeler
Katherine & Michael Yates

BOUNDARY-BREAKERS
Katie Bradford
Tim Fosberry

MOVER-SHAKERS
Anonymous
John & Annoushka Ayton
Cas & Philip Donald
Duncan Matthews QC
The David & Elaine Potter Charitable Foundation
Ian & Carol Sellars
Jan & Michael Topham

HISTORY-MAKERS
Jack & Linda Keenan*
Miles Morland

MAJOR DONORS
Rob & Siri Cope
Daniel & Joanna Friel
Deborah & Stephen Marquardt
Lady Sainsbury of Turville
Nora Lee & Jon Sedmak*
The Williams Charitable Trust

*Supporters of the American Friends of the Royal Court (AFRCT)

FOR THE ROYAL COURT

info@royalcourttheatre.com, www.royalcourttheatre.com
Royal Court Theatre, Sloane Square, London SW1W 8AS
Tel: 020 7565 5050 Fax: 020 7565 5001

Artistic Director **Dominic Cooke**
Deputy Artistic Director **Jeremy Herrin**
Associate Director **Sacha Wares***
Artistic Associate **Emily McLaughlin***
Diversity Associate **Ola Animashawun***
Education Associate **Lynne Gagliano***
Producer **Vanessa Stone***

Literary Manager **Ruth Little**
Senior Reader **Nicola Wass****
Literary Assistant **Marcelo Dos Santos**

Studio Administrator **Clare McQuillan**
Writers' Tutor **Leo Butler***

Associate Director International **Elyse Dodgson**
International Projects Manager **Chris James**
International Assistant **William Drew**

Casting Director (Maternity Cover) **Julia Horan**
Casting Director **Amy Ball**
Casting Assistant **Lotte Hines**

Head of Production **Paul Handley**
JTU Production Manager **Tariq Rifaat**
Production Administrator **Sarah Davies**
Head of Lighting **Matt Drury**
Lighting Deputy **Stephen Andrews**
Lighting Assistant **Katie Pitt**
Lighting Board Operator **Tom Lightbody**
Head of Stage **Steven Stickler**
Stage Deputy **Duncan Russell**
Stage Chargehand **Lee Crimmen**
Chargehand Carpenter **Richard Martin**
Head of Sound **David McSeveney**
Sound Deputy **Alex Caplen**
Head of Costume **Iona Kenrick**
Costume Deputy **Jackie Orton**
Wardrobe Assistant **Pam Anson**

Executive Director **Kate Horton**
Head of Finance & Administration **Helen Perryer**
Planning Administrator **Davina Shah**
Production Assistant **David Nock**
Senior Finance & Administration Officer **Martin Wheeler**
Finance Officer **Rachel Harrison***
Finance & Administration Assistant **Tessa Rivers**
Head of Communications **Kym Bartlett**
Marketing Manager **Becky Wootton**
Press & Public Relations Officer **Anna Evans**
Communications Assistant **Ruth Hawkins**
Communications Intern **Caroline Morris**
Education/Marketing Intern **Cheri Davies**
Sales Manager **Kevin West**
Deputy Sales Manager **Daniel Alicandro**
Box Office Sales Assistants **Cheryl Gallacher**,
Ciara O'Toole, **Richard Hart***, **Helen Murray***,
Natalia Tarjanyi*, **Amanda Wilkin***

Head of Development **Gaby Styles**
Senior Development Manager **Hannah Clifford**
Trusts & Foundations Manager **Khalila Hassouna**
Development Officer **Lucy Buxton**
Development Assistant **Penny Saward**
US Fundraising Counsel **Tim Runion**
Development Intern **Helen Shutt**

Theatre Manager **Bobbie Stokes**
Deputy Theatre Manager **Daniel O'Neill**
Front of House Manager **Siobhan Lightfoot**
Duty Managers **Stuart Grey***, **Claire Simpson***
Bar & Food Manager **Baljinder Kalirai**
Events Manager **Joanna Ostrom**
Assistant Bar & Food Manager **Sami Rifaat**
Head Chef **Charlie Brookman**
Bookshop Manager **Simon David**
Assistant Bookshop Manager **Edin Suljic***
Bookshop Assistant **Vanessa Hammick** *
Customer Service Assistant **Deidre Lennon***
Stage Door/Reception **Simon David***,
Paul Lovegrove, Tyrone Lucas

Thanks to all of our box office assistants, ushers and bar staff.

** The post of Senior Reader is supported by Nora Lee & Jon Sedmak through the American Friends of the Royal Court Theatre.

* Part-time.

ENGLISH STAGE COMPANY

President
Dame Joan Plowright CBE

Honorary Council
Sir Richard Eyre CBE
Alan Grieve CBE
Martin Paisner CBE

Council
Chairman **Anthony Burton**
Vice Chairman **Graham Devlin CBE**

Members
Jennette Arnold
Judy Daish
Sir David Green KCMG
Joyce Hytner OBE
Stephen Jeffreys
Wasfi Kani OBE
Phyllida Lloyd CBE
James Midgley
Sophie Okonedo
Alan Rickman
Anita Scott
Katharine Viner
Stewart Wood

DRUM THEATRE
PLYMOUTH THEATRES

"At Plymouth they are maximizing the potential of those who could be the great theatre-makers of tomorrow...You only have to look around British theatre to see the Drum's fingerprints everywhere."
THE GUARDIAN

The Drum Theatre produces and presents new plays. As part of the Theatre Royal Plymouth we have built a national reputation for the quality of our programme and innovative work, winning the Peter Brook Empty Space Award in 2007. We often collaborate with other leading theatres and companies like the Royal Court, including, most recently, ATC, Told by an Idiot, the Lyric Hammersmith, Frantic Assembly and the Belgian company, Ontroerend Goed.

"Now, under Simon Stokes, Plymouth has become a magnet for talent."
THE OBSERVER

In 2009 we commissioned and produced Chris Goode's play about Edward Lear, *King Pelican*. We co-produced a new experimental work, *Under the Influence*, with Ontroerend Goed for production in Plymouth and Ghent, before touring internationally in 2010. Working with Told by an Idiot for the first time, we co-produced an adaptation of Michel Faber's *The Fahrenheit Twins* for national touring and a run at the Barbican Centre, London. We've had major success with a new 'horror' play, *Grand Guignol*, commissioned from Kneehigh's writer and performer, Carl Grose. The Theatre Royal's Young Company and People's Company, based at TR2, also perform in the Drum Theatre.

"What would British Theatre do without the Drum?"
THE GUARDIAN

DRUM THEATRE
PLYMOUTH THEATRES

TR2, our production and education centre, is a truly unique facility. This architecturally award-winning building contains unrivalled set, costume, prop-making and rehearsal facilities. Some of our most important and vigorous work is carried out here by our Creative Learning team, who provide one of the most comprehensive education and outreach programmes in the UK.

"Not many organisations in Plymouth can claim to have international standing, appeal to thousands of people of all ages from across the city and beyond, put our city on the cultural map and have consistently punched way above their weight for 26 star spangled years: yet this is the proud achievement of Plymouth's Theatre Royal, which plays such a major part in our city's cultural life."

THE PLYMOUTH HERALD

Chairman - **Sir Michael Lickiss**
Chief Executive - **Adrian Vinken OBE**
Artistic Director - **Simon Stokes**
General Manager - **Alvin Hargreaves**
Acting Director of Production - **David Miller**
Finance Director - **Paul James**
Marketing & Sales Director - **Marianne Locatori**
Creative Learning Director - **Victoria Allen**
Theatre Manager - **Jack Mellor**
Artistic Associate - **David Prescott**
Production Manager - **Nick Soper**
Technical Coordinator - **Mark Hawker**
Wardrobe Manager - **Dina Hall**
Interim Workshop Managers - **David Elliot, Sebastian Soper**
PR Manager - **Anne-Marie Clark (01752 230479)**

Box Office - **01752 267222**
www.theatreroyal.com

Registered Charity Number 284545

Plymouth

Supported by
**ARTS COUNCIL
ENGLAND**

The Empire

'Our thoughts move across the sea to the many communities in which our people play their part, in every corner of the world. These are our family ties. That is our life. Without it, we should be no more than some millions of people living on an island off the coast of Europe, in which nobody wants to take any particular interest.'

Sir Anthony Eden, then Foreign Secretary (1952)

'The conquest of the earth . . . is not a pretty thing when you look into it much. What redeems it is an idea only. An idea at the back of it; not a sentimental pretence but an idea; and an unselfish belief in the idea – something you can set up, and bow down before, and offer a sacrifice to . . .'

Marlow, in Joseph Conrad's
Heart of Darkness (1902)

Characters

Gary
Hafizullah
Jalandar
Simon
Zia

Notes on the play

Gary and Simon are British soldiers, part of an operational mentoring and liaison team (OMLT), working with the Afghan National Army (ANA) in the Helmand Province of Afghanistan in the summer of 2006. Hafizullah and Jalandar are both serving members of the ANA.

Gary, Jalandar, Simon and Zia should all have healthy beards. Hafizullah should have barely any facial hair.

Summer 2006.

An empty room, part of an abandoned compound in a remote region of the Helmand Province of Afghanistan.

Fierce sunlight / heat outside.

*Enter **Gary**, an unarmed British soldier, wearing white plastic gloves. He peers in through the doorless entrance and considers the room.*

Gary Yeah, in here.

He turns round: the person he thought he was talking to isn't there.

Where's he . . . ? (*Spotting him outside in the distance.*) Paddy! What the fuck are you . . . ? *Oi! Oi, Paddy!* This way! In here. (*Pause.*) No. *No. This way.*

A pause, during which he sighs, shakes his head and exits. As he goes, we hear him say to himself:

Dozy cunt.

A longish pause before we hear:

(*Off.*) Come on, hurry up, you bender.

A pause before we hear:

(*Off.*) You get that end. No, no, with your knees. You're gonna. No, with your *knees*. You're gonna. Yeah, that's it. Come on.

Gary *and* **Hafizullah** *enter on: 'Come on.'* **Gary** *and* **Hafizullah** *– an unarmed, uniformed Afghan soldier – are at either end of a sheet of material, which they're using to carry a dirtied and bloodied body. The body is dressed in local traditional dress (shalwar kameez, etc.) and appears lifeless.*

Gary God, he ain't light.

They rest the body in the centre of the room.

Is he? For the size of it.

Hafizullah *looks like he's only just woken up. He shrugs at **Gary**'s question and vaguely inspects the body, having seen its face for the first time.*

Gary Yeah, should be OK there, out the fucking. Sun.

A pause during which **Gary** *notices that* **Hafizullah** *is continuing to hang over the body.*

Gary What ya doing?

Hafizullah *gestures with his head to the body.*

Hafizullah Him.

Gary Yeah, what about him?

Hafizullah Punjabi.

Gary Punwhat?

Hafizullah Punjabi. From Pakistan.

Gary Is he?

Hafizullah *nods.*

Gary Right.

He nods in turn.

Pause.

How can ya like, tell?

Hafizullah His face.

Gary OK, yeah, suppose he does look a bit more.

He gestures vaguely to his own face.

A pause as they both look down and consider the body.

Whatever he is, he's a bit fat, inny? Not fat fat, but for a Terry. (*Doing a slight bloated gesture.*) You know. Fat.

Hafizullah *looks blankly at* **Gary**.

Gary No?

Hafizullah *shrugs.*

Gary *looks around the room a little.*

Gary   Right. Alright, I'm dry as a cunt here. Just gonna go and get some water. So, while I'm gone, don't let no one come in, apart from my lot, alright? (*Gesturing with two fingers.*) I'll be two seconds.

Hafizullah *nods.*

Gary   Alright?

Hafizullah *nods.*

Gary   Good. Good lad.

He gives a double 'thumbs up' to **Hafizullah***.*

Hafizullah *half smiles in response and nods.*

Gary *exits, throwing his gloves down on the ground as he goes.*

Hafizullah *looks at the gloves on the ground before looking around the room. He then sits down in one of the corners of the room nearest to the doorway. He takes out a little tin and starts to construct a fairly modest joint, humming a Hindi pop tune to himself – moving his head and body slightly to its rhythm – as he does so.*

Suddenly the body stirs/moves/groans. **Hafizullah** *stops humming/ rolling and looks towards it, mildly concerned/bothered. He then looks to the doorway (hoping for some sign of* **Gary***), before looking back at the body.* **Hafizullah** *continues looking but there is no further movement/ sound and he is eventually able to go – tentatively – back to humming/ rolling, but is a bit quieter in doing so.*

After a short while **Gary** *enters – in a little bit of a rush, a little breathless – carrying two bottles of water. He gives one of these to* **Hafizullah** *and then goes back and stands in the doorway, looking out.*

Hafizullah *gives* **Gary** *a single, slightly pathetic 'thumbs up' – in thanks for the water – as he receives the bottle. Almost in unison,* **Gary** *clocks that* **Hafizullah** *is rolling a joint and shakes his head a little at the predictability/ridiculousness of this.*

Gary   Your lot rocked up.

They are in his sightline outside. He gestures to them.

Out front.

Hafizullah *stops rolling the joint.*

Hafizullah   What?

Gary   ANA. About ten of 'em just drove in, two wagons. (*Referring to the body.*) Must have heard about. (*Watching the ANA.*) Look like they got a right mood on.

Hafizullah   Mood?

Gary (*translating*)   Look. You know. Angry.

Hafizullah   Yes?

Gary *nods.*

Gary (*still watching events outside*)   About him though, I reckon, not you. And don't worry, I'll cover for ya, if there is any bother, 'bout you going AWOL 'n that.

Hafizullah, *a little reassured, nods.*

Gary   If they notice. Or care. They're just there talking to, to Rupert. Over the way.

Hafizullah *nods a little but doesn't get up to take a look.*

A long pause as **Gary** *continues to watch the scene outside in the distance, drinking from the bottle as he does so.*

Gary   Yeah. Yeah, no, they're heading off.

Hafizullah   Gone?

Gary *nods.*

Gary   Well, going. Musta got the message. There's a first.

Hafizullah *nods.*

Content the ANA are leaving, **Gary** *moves back into the room. He rests back against the wall, very close to the doorway, though during the following dialogue he occasionally peers back to see what's going on.*

He exhales and takes a few more sips of water. **Hafizullah** *starts again on making the joint.*

Gary   Fucking. Hot. Innit?

Hafizullah *nods.*

Hafizullah   Yes.

Gary   I know it's the desert but still. Fucking.

He shakes his head, exhales and possibly wafts the air.

A longish pause.

How do you, like, live in it?

Hafizullah   Hot.

Gary   Yeah, yeah, I'm saying. How do you live in it? Like, day-to-day?

Hafizullah *shrugs.*

Gary   Cos you ain't that much darker than me.

No response.

So how d'ya fucking cope with it?

A pause, before **Hafizullah** *shrugs.*

Hafizullah   . . .

Gary   Right. Right. Suppose the art of conversation must help you through it.

Hafizullah   What?

Gary   Nothing, don't . . .

Hafizullah   . . . ?

Gary   Don't matter: I'm being a cunt.

He gestures for **Hafizullah** *to forget it.*

Hafizullah *nods.* **Gary** *nods.*

Gary *exhales/ sighs.*

A long pause, at the start of which **Hafizullah** *lights his joint.*

The smell of the smoke starts to hit **Gary**.

Gary   God, what is in that?

He wafts the smoke away.

Gary   Smells like. Fucking. (*Sniffs.*) Orh.

Hafizullah *coughs a little.* **Gary** *coughs as well.*

Gary   Jesus.

He watches **Hafizullah** *take another drag.*

He shakes his head.

Gary   You really must be some lucky bastard.

Hafizullah *shrugs and starts to laugh a little.*

Gary (*smiling a bit*)   Like, that shit'd send me out. Can barely speak, let alone fucking. Fight. Shoot straight.

Hafizullah   It helps me. Sleep.

Gary   Yeah?

Hafizullah   Yes.

Gary   Well, that's useful. On a battlefield.

Hafizullah   Yes.

Gary *shakes his head.*

Pause.

Gary   My brother Matty, he's a bit like that.

Hafizullah   What?

Gary   Can't sleep – can't do nothing – without a bit o'.

He makes a 'smoking a joint' gesture.

Hafizullah *nods.*

Hafizullah   It turns off your head.

Gary   Yeah?

Hafizullah *nods.*

Gary   Well, Matty ain't got much to turn off, so must work a fucking treat.

Hafizullah   What?

Gary   He's a dozy prick, like you.

Hafizullah *nods.*

Gary *nods.*

Pause.

Gary   Though, your English is better.

Hafizullah   No.

Gary   Yeah. Well, no, but he talks like he's fucking. Black or summat. Before I came out here – this tour – he started calling me 'bredren'.

He shakes his head.

Hafizullah   Bread?

Gary   Can you believe that?

Hafizullah   What?

Gary   I mean, I probably got more in common with you than him. Apart from the puff stuff. How d'ya learn?

Hafizullah   What?

Gary   English.

Hafizullah   Yes. My mother was. Teacher.

Gary   Yeah?

Hafizullah *nods.*

Hafizullah   Yes.

Gary   What she teach?

Hafizullah   History. English. All things.

Gary   Wow.

Hafizullah *nods.*

Gary   Cool.

Hafizullah   Yes.

Gary   I'm having lessons. Learning. (*Gesturing to* **Hafizullah**.) Dari, 'n that.

Hafizullah   You?

Gary *nods.*

Gary   Oh yeah. Fucking. Difficult. Innit?

Pause.

Hafizullah   Say something.

Gary   What?

Hafizullah   In Dari.

Gary   Na.

Hafizullah *nods.*

Gary   Na, mate. I'll just. Fuck it up.

Hafizullah *gestures for him to say something.*

Hafizullah   Please.

Gary   OK. OK then.

He considers.

Alright. *Ismi man* Gary *hast.*

Hafizullah   Yes. Yes. 'My name is Gary.'

He nods, really pleased with this.

Gary   Yeah. Didn't sound, wrong or nothing?

Hafizullah   No. Good.

Gary   Right.

Hafizullah *gestures for more.*

Hafizullah   More.

Gary   Another? Erm. OK. *Tashnob kujost?* (*With a noticeable emphasis on 'nob'.*)

Hafizullah   Good, good. 'Where is the bathroom?'

Gary   Exactly, yeah, bang on.

Hafizullah (*gesturing to the empty room, playing along*)   'I don't know. It is gone.'

Gary   Yeah.

Hafizullah   'Empty.'

Gary *nods.*

Hafizullah *nods, smiling.*

Pause.

Gary   That's about it so far, so all I can do is find a toilet and then introduce myself. Or the other way round. Neither of which is very . . . Unless I go cottaging. Gonna keep it up though, I reckon: Dari. I'd love to be like fluent 'n that. Billingual, yeah, like you.

Hafizullah *nods.*

Gary   That'd be awesome.

Hafizullah   My mother, could speak five language.

Gary   Five?

Hafizullah *nods.*

Gary   Fuck.

Hafizullah   Yes.

Gary   That's, four and a half more than Matty.

Hafizullah *nods, not really getting this.*

They share a smile.

Gary   Well. Well done. Well done, Mum.

He raises his bottle of water in a toast.

Hafizullah *raises his own bottle.*

Gary   Cheers.

Hafizullah *nods.*

They both drink.

Gary   Yep. Yes.

He sighs.

A pause, during which **Hafizullah** *– having put the cap back on his water – looks a little down/distracted.*

Gary   You alright?

Hafizullah *nods, not entirely convincingly, and takes another drag.*

Gary   Sure?

Hafizullah *nods, breathing out smoke, still looking a little troubled/distant.*

A long pause.

Gary *(trying Geordie)*   'Day three in the Big Brother house.'

Hafizullah   . . .

Gary   . . .

Pause.

Tell ya what, if the bullets don't kill ya, the waiting will.

Hafizullah   . . .

Gary   As they say.

Enter **Jalandar***, a young, uniformed ANA soldier armed with a Kalashnikov hung over his shoulder.*

Jalandar *walks straight up to the body and starts to urinate on it; also gives the body a little kick as he does so.*

Gary   Oi, what the fuck do you think you're . . . ?

He moves round in front of **Jalandar** *to stop him. In the process,* **Jalandar** *ends up pissing over* **Gary***.*

Gary   Ah! *You dirty cunt!* That's fucking . . . *Oh . . . Oh God. Look at that.*

He brushes himself down and shoves **Jalandar** *back to the doorway, away from the body.*

Gary   Go on, over there. Fucking . . . (*Referring to his piss-stained uniform, holding it up, smelling it.*) Oh, that is . . . that is *horrendous.*

Jalandar   Taliban.

Gary   *Yeah* – yeah – but that don't mean you can fucking . . . walk in here and be all . . .

Jalandar (*smiling, referring to his crotch*)   Piss. (*Referring to his Kalashnikov.*) Shoot.

He shrugs.

(*In Dari, to* **Hafizullah**)   'Will he let me shoot him?'

Gary   . . . ?

Hafizullah *shrugs.*

Gary   What's he saying?

Hafizullah   Why you not . . . ?

Jalandar *spits at the body.*

Gary   *Oi,* will you stop it?! What you gonna do next, have a fucking dump on him?

Jalandar   Taliban.

Gary   I don't care, *stop it.*

Jalandar   Shoot?

He starts to take his Kalashnikov off his shoulder.

Gary   No. No.

Jalandar   He is . . . Talib?

Gary   Yeah, but . . .

Jalandar   Then. Shoot.

Gary   *No.*

Jalandar   Why no?

Gary   Because . . . he's . . . because he's getting medical treatment from our lot before . . .

Jalandar   . . . ?

Gary   . . . before your lot can do . . . do your magic, alright? So, later on, you can . . . shit on him, use his cock as a toothbrush – I don't care – but *now*, you can't. Now, you have to piss off.

Jalandar   Piss?

Gary   *No.* No more o' that. Keep it in the lair.

Jalandar   Shoot?

Gary   Fuck sake. You can later. Now. Jog on.

He gestures for **Jalandar** *to leave.*

Jalandar *looks at him blankly.*

Gary   Look, I know your English is a bit fucking shit but I ain't telling you again. And I think I'm being pretty fucking polite given that you've just pissed all over me. So there's the door – well, where there should be a door – now use it.

Pause.

Gary *gives him a look.*

Jalandar   OK. OK.

Jalandar *nods a little, smiles at them, spits on the ground and exits.*

Gary *moves towards the doorway and watches him as he leaves, making sure* **Jalandar** *will stay gone.*

Gary *exhales.*

Gary   Fuck sake. (*Feeling his uniform, having a sniff.*) Arh, that is gonna reek later.

He shakes his head in disbelief. Looks back out to where **Jalandar** *went.*

Gary   He's a fucking . . . animal, inny?

Hafizullah *shrugs.*

Gary   Imagine what he'd do to the fucker, if we weren't.

Hafizullah *shrugs, looking a little down/distracted.*

Pause.

Gary   On that. Why haven't you, like, tried to hurt him or nothing? I know you're soft 'n that, but he's still a fucking.

Hafizullah   I am lover, not fighter.

He smiles, having cheered himself up a bit with his own joke.

Gary   Yeah? Are ya?

Hafizullah *nods.*

Hafizullah   Yes.

Gary (*smiling a bit*)   Right. No, you're a bell-end is what you are, mate.

Hafizullah *smiling, shrugs.*

Gary (*smiling*)   Yes. You are.

A pause during which he sees someone approaching outside.

God, talking of which.

Hafizullah   What?

Gary (*gestures with his head*)   Rupert.

Shaking his head, he retreats back into the room as the figure approaches.

Cometh the hour.

He coughs, clears his throat.

After a short while, **Simon** *arrives, an unarmed British soldier. He stands at the edge of the doorway, peering in.*

Simon   Everything OK?

Gary *nods.*

Hafizullah *also nods, though he and* **Simon** *can't yet see each other.*

Pause.

Simon   This heat.

Gary   Innit.

Simon   Could melt your teeth. I didn't think you could actually get hotter than Basra.

Gary *nods/half smiles.*

Pause.

Simon (*referring to* **Jalandar**)   So what was our friend after?

Gary   You know, like: first dibs.

Simon   Thought as much.

He shakes his head.

Gary *nods.*

Simon   I told them to steer clear, I did. I was pretty fucking. Explicit.

Gary   Right.

Simon   Radioed their commander.

Gary *nods.*

Gary   Yeah.

Simon   Raised a bit of hell. But there's always one.

Gary *nods. Coughs.*

Simon   Isn't there?

Gary   Yes, sir.

Simon   Especially out here. Like herding cats.

Gary *nods. Sniffs. Clears his throat. Nods.*

Pause.

Gary (*gesturing to someone outside*)   So how's . . . ? How's he doing?

Simon   Um. Yeah. Yeah, he's . . .

Gary   Still can't believe he fucking like, walked away from it, like that.

Simon *nods.*

Simon   Yeah. He's . . . Yeah.

Gary   Mental. Any word on the Chinook?

Simon *shakes his head.*

Simon   Not yet, no. (*Pause. Gesturing to the body.*) Let's have a look at Terrence then.

Gary   Yeah, he might be a bit. Damp.

Simon   What?

Gary   Nothing. sir. Here ya are.

He moves out of the way of the body.

Simon (*this was obvious*)   Yeah.

He moves into the room; as he does so, spots **Hafizullah** *in the corner.*

Simon   Hello.

Hafizullah   Yes.

Simon (*to* **Gary**)   Who . . . ? Who is this?

Gary   Paddy.

Simon   Paddy?

Hafizullah   Yes.

He nods.

Gary   Yeah. Well, that's . . . that's what I call him, yeah.

Simon   OK, and . . . what's he doing? In here?

Gary   I . . . Well . . . I found him, having a kip in the orchard round the back. Snoring his head off, didn't even have a rifle or nothing. Yeah, probably sold it for a pair of socks.

Gary *snorts/ laughs a bit.*

Simon   And?

Gary   Oh. Er. Yeah. He was out with the ANA during the main contact today but he musta got a bit sick and tired of all the running around and being a soldier. Stuff.

Simon *gestures 'so what?'.*

Gary   But it's alright, I know him from their compound 'n that and I needed an extra pair of hands anyway so I just thought. He's alright, honestly, sir. Speaks good English. Can translate, if we want him to. He really helped me out with all the . . . with the guy who just come in here.

He nods.

Yeah. Very helpful.

Simon   But we already have a translator. Namir.

Gary   Yeah.

Simon   And . . . what about having him in here with?

He gestures to the body.

Gary   Yeah, no, he wouldn't hurt a fly, sir. Well, he might try and smoke it but I vouch for him. Definitely. Hundred per cent. Two hundred per cent.

Simon   Right.

Gary   Yep.

Simon   OK. Just don't. Don't leave him alone with.

Gary   No. Course not. Wouldn't do that.

He shakes his head.

Unprofessional.

He nods.

In the background, **Hafizullah** *either relights his old joint or starts on a new one.* **Gary** *clocks this.*

Simon   I mean, however much you . . . He's still ANA.

Gary   Yes, sir.

Simon   And I'm not having him. Hurt.

Gary   No, sir. (*Pause.*) Though.

Simon   Though?

Gary   Well. He will be.

Simon   Will be what?

Gary   Hurt. When they do. Like. Get him 'n that.

Simon *briefly turns and looks at* **Hafizullah**.

Simon   Possibly.

Gary   So . . .

Simon   . . . ?

Gary   So. What's the point, patching him first, if they're just gonna fuck him up later? I don't really understand. The point of it, to be honest, sir. Waste of bandages. Innit?

Simon   Well.

Gary   Sir.

Simon   Corporal.

Gary   What?

Simon   You don't need to understand. Though it is pretty simple. If you think about it.

Pause.

Gary   Er. Yes, sir.

Simon *looks at* **Gary**.

He nods.

Simon   Yeah.

They share a stare. **Gary** *looks down first.*

Gary   Just like to be out there. Help out. That's all.

Simon   Of course. But you can't.

A pause, during which he starts to smell something.

Is that . . . ? Is he smoking . . . hash?

Gary   Possibly.

Simon   Right.

He nods.

OK. OK. Well then. (*Pause.*) Well. 'Crack on.'

He looks at both **Gary** *and* **Hafizullah***, shakes his head and then exits.*

After a brief pause, **Gary** *moves towards the doorway and watches* **Simon** *walk away.*

During **Gary***'s next few lines of dialogue, the body on the ground starts to stir and groans slightly.* **Hafizullah** *notices this in the corner of his vision.*

Gary   Brilliant. (*Doing a ridiculously posh voice.*) 'Is he smoking hash?' Quick, inny? No wonder he got all them fucking. A levels.

Hafizullah (*returning his focus to* **Gary** *but still with a bit of an eye on the body*)   What?

Gary   Just saying he's like. Educated 'n that.

Hafizullah *nods.*

Hafizullah   Yes?

Gary   Yeah. Posh.

Hafizullah   What is, posh?

Gary   Him.

He nods, still looking out in the direction that **Simon** *went.*

Hafizullah (*under his breath, looking at the body*)   Posh.

Gary   Yeah, they all are.

Hafizullah   Who?

Gary   Fucking.

Zia   Oh my days.

Hafizullah *looks back to the body –* **Zia**.

Gary   Top brass. (*Turning to* **Hafizullah**, *thinking it was him speaking*.) Oh your what?

Zia *groans/moves, as he awakens slightly.*

Hafizullah *gestures towards* **Zia**.

Gary (*to* **Hafizullah**)   What ya say?

Hafizullah   Him.

Zia   My leg.

Gary   . . . ?

Hafizullah *gestures towards* **Zia**.

Hafizullah   Him.

Gary   Did he just . . . ?

Hafizullah *nods.*

Zia   Oh my gosh.

Gary   . . . fucking . . . ?

Hafizullah   . . .

He nods slowly.

Zia *groans before slipping back into unconsciousness.*

A stunned silence, during which **Gary** *and* **Hafizullah** *stare at* **Zia**.

Gary   He did. He just . . .

Hafizullah *nods.*

Hafizullah   Yes.

Gary *looks intently at* **Zia** *for a while before reaching down and throwing the rest of his bottle of water over* **Zia***'s head.*

Zia *wakes up with a start.*

Zia   What you doing, bruv?

Blinking and spluttering, **Zia** *opens his eyes for the first time and pushes himself awkwardly (getting searing pain from his leg and shouting 'Ah fuck' and other expletives as he does so) towards the back wall, which is opposite the doorway and which he leans back against.*

Gary   I'm fucking . . . water.

Zia   What?

Gary   'Bruv.'

Zia   Ah . . . my leg.

He wipes his face dry on his sleeve and then, gradually, recovering from the shooting pain in his leg, fully opens his eyes, gathers his breath and takes in the room. Only then does he look for the first time properly at both **Gary** *and* **Hafizullah**.

A moment as they all consider each other.

Zia   . . .

Gary   . . .

Zia *(to both of them)*   Who . . . who are you?

Gary   No.

Zia   And what you . . . what you doing?

Gary   No.

Gary *and* **Zia** *stare at each other.*

Gary   You are. *You're* . . . ?

Hafizullah   English.

Gary *clicks the fingers of one hand at* **Hafizullah** *and nods.*

Zia *nods.*

Gary   Right.

Zia   Yeah.

Gary   Fucking . . .

Zia (*getting a shooting pain in his leg*)   Arh. What's . . . ah *fuck*, what's . . . what's up with my leg?

Gary   Broken.

Zia   Hurts.

Gary *nods.*

Gary   Yeah, it'll do that.

Zia   And it's all . . . wet.

Gary   Yeah. So how . . . ? What . . . ?

He steadies himself a little.

Right. OK. Alright. Alright. OK.

Zia   What?

Gary   Let's. Let's. OK. Let's. Start. With the start.

Zia (*getting another shooting pain in his leg*)   Arh.

Gary   Let's . . .

Zia (*gesturing to his plasticuffs*)   And wha's this about?

Gary   That's to stop you . . . fucking . . . No, no – actually, right? – you aren't . . . you're not *asking* questions here, mate. That's not . . . that's not how it's gonna fucking work, OK? Let's establish that *now*.

Zia   OK, I'm . . .

Gary   *Yeah?*

Zia   OK.

He nods.

Gary   Good. Good. Then. Let's . . . Like I say. Let's, start with the start and don't . . . don't mess me around or, or *talk*, or ask any more stupid fucking questions. You got that? . . . ?

A pause before **Zia** *nods.*

Gary   Excellent. Fantastic. Excellent.

He exhales.

Pause.

So what the fuck?

Zia   What?

Gary   You heard.

Pause.

He gestures for **Zia** *to answer.*

Gary   Come on then.

Zia   Yeah but. That's not really a. Proper question.

Gary   Yeah it is.

Zia   But . . . how . . . how am I meant ta . . . ?

Gary   Answer.

Zia   . . . ?

Gary   I mean it.

Zia   Answer . . . what?

Gary   What. The fuck?

Zia   I'm . . . Look, I'm . . . I speak English, yeah, but I don't think I'm fluent in whatever dialect you . . . I don't get what . . . what you're . . .

Gary   Because I was expecting some fucked-up farmboy. Some local. (*Pointing to* **Hafizullah**.) Punjabi, whatever. Not . . . You. So what the fuck?

Zia   OK. OK. I see that you . . . why . . . why you would . . . why you wanna . . . All it is, yeah? I'm . . . I've been . . .

Gary   No, no, fuck that actually. First off. Proper, first off. (*A pause as he composes himself.*) Important. What's your name?

Zia   Look.

Gary   What?

Zia   Look.

Gary   Well, that's a shit name, innit? Look. What's your surname? Up?

Zia   No. No.

He shakes his head.

Gary   No? So what is it then? I'd ask your rank but. (*Pause.*) What, playing it all cool, is we?

Zia   No.

Gary   So what the fuck is your name, son?

Pause.

Zia   OK. OK.

Gary   Yeah?

Zia   OK. (*Pause.*) Zia.

Gary   What?

Zia   Zia.

Gary   . . . ?

He shakes his head.

Zia   *Zia.* Z-I-A. Rhymes with, Leah, yeah, but with a Z. Zia.

Gary   Zia?

Zia   Yeah.

Gary   Well, Zia. With a 'Z'. Fucking. Pleasure.

Zia   . . .

Gary   Ain't it, Paddy?

Hafizullah   . . .

Gary   Cos we was getting all lonely. But now:

He gestures to **Zia**, *as if to say: 'Now you're here.'*

He nods.

Gary   Well, let's return the honours then. I'm Gary and that's Paddy there. In the corner.

Hafizullah   Yes.

Zia   OK. OK. Nice to. To meet you.

Gary *scoffs.*

Gary   Is it?

Zia *shrugs.*

Zia   I . . .

Gary   Whatever, now . . . now that we've been introduced – pleasantries – you can explain to us, what the fuck you're doing here.

Zia   Look.

Gary   Can't ya?

Zia   I'm . . . Look, I don't know what . . .

Gary   What . . . ?

Zia   I don't know what you're thinking here, yeah, but . . .

Gary   Thinking? Thinking's above my pay grade, mate.

Zia   OK, well, look, I'm not . . .

Gary   Not . . . ?

Zia   I ain't . . . I don't know what's going on here though, yeah?

Gary   Join the club.

Hafizullah   He is, English?

Gary   *Yes*, Paddy.

Zia Look.

Gary (*directed at* **Hafizullah**) Fuck sake. (*At* **Zia**.) Look?
What at?

Zia No. Look.

Gary Stop – look – stop just saying fucking 'look'.

Zia Sorry. I'm . . . I'm sorry. Look. Listen. Listen, to me.
I just, I just think you should maybe like calm down a bit,
yeah?

Gary Oh really?

Zia *nods.*

Zia Yeah. Yeah. You got me . . . You got me all tied up. For
some reason.

Gary Yeah.

Zia And my leg is . . .

Gary *nods.*

Zia *nods in turn.*

Zia So. I ain't going nowhere. You can see that and you
don't need to be all like . . . You can. Chill out, you know
that?

Gary Chill out? Can I fucking really?

Zia *nods.*

Zia That's what I'm saying to you.

Gary Well, you know, I'm totally chill. To the max, bruv.
Like a fucking. Pimp-daddy.

Zia I'm . . . OK, but you don't seem like it that much and
I wanna let you know I'm not . . .

Gary Not . . . ?

Zia I'm not . . .

Gary . . . ?

Zia   Whatever you must like. Think.

Gary   Told ya, I ain't paid enough to *think*.

Zia   Yeah, well, you must think something cos, why else you got me like this? And why you looking at me like that? Like you wanna rip my. Head off.

He gestures, as if to say, 'Well?'

Pause.

Gary   OK. Alright then. OK. I think, I think – Zia – I think that you tried to kill me and my mates today – but that you fucked it up, royally – and that now, you're gonna pay for that.

He smiles and nods.

Zia *laughs nervously.*

Gary   Ain't he, Paddy?

Zia   What?

Hafizullah   What?

Gary   Yeah. So you were right: I do think something. Well done.

Zia   OK. OK. This is . . . This ain't making . . . Look. I don't what you're talking about, yeah? And you look pretty vexed at me so, so I believe that you believe that, what you just said – I do – but I wasn't . . . I ain't some . . .

Gary   Some . . . ?

Zia   No. No way.

Gary   Some *what*?

Zia   I'm not, I'm telling you that now, bruv.

Gary   Some? What?

Zia   I dunno. Like. (*Pause.*) Bad guy.

Gary   No?

Zia   No.

Pause.

Gary   So what are ya then?

Zia   Look. I'm. I'm on . . .

Gary   What you even talking about?

Zia   I'm . . . Yeah, I'm on. Please. I'm on holiday.

Gary   . . . ? What?

Zia   Yeah. Holiday, bruv.

He nods.

Gary *scoffs.*

Gary   What, you take a wrong turning before Ibiza?

Zia   No – no – that's not what, I'm not . . .

Gary   Fair enough, I can see how that would happen. It is very hot, there's a lot sand about and I did spot – the other day – a building round the way that looks just like Manumission.

Zia   Not. No. Not that kinda holiday.

Gary   Oh really?

Zia   Yeah, but just let me explain this to you and you will understand, believe that.

Gary   OK then. OK. Try me. Go on.

Gary *gestures for him to 'out with it'.*

Zia   I told you. I'm telling you. Thank you. Thank you, mate. Thank you. (*Pause.*) I'm on holiday. I'm on. And it wasn't like a piss-up or nothing – I don't drink or do none of that, yeah? Though, though I used to, back in the day, I was a bit of a boy, yeah? But, but not now though, no way, cut it all out, started going to the gym, all this, proper detox, like my body is . . . now, I'm like . . . So yeah, it was just meant to be like a quiet family holiday thing this time. Went to Pakistan first and I just came over with some, some business.

Gary   What, like jihad business?

Zia   No, no, just let me talk, yeah? Explain this to you.
Honestly.

Gary   OK. OK. Talk. Fucking . . . *Talk*. Explain. Explain
honestly how you end up on a battlefield, with an AK-47 at
your feet, slap bang in the middle of where that ambush come
from. Dressed up like some . . . (*He gestures to* **Zia***'s clothes.*)
Yeah, talk.

Zia   Where you getting that? I didn't have no . . .

Gary   No? Cos Butcher found you himself and he told me
himself and I'm more inclined to believe a fucking Sergeant
Major over some little –

Zia   I don't know *nothing* about . . .

Gary   Course not.

Zia   I mean, it might have been in the general, like, area but
it weren't . . . mine.

Gary   Convenient.

Zia   Not really, is it?

Gary   So how'd it get there? Magic?

Zia   It musta, yeah, it musta belonged to the guys who like.
Kidnapped me.

Gary   Hang on.

Zia   One of them.

Gary   Hold up. *Kidnapped?*

Zia *nods.*

Zia   Yeah, I was . . .

Gary   By . . . ? By who?

Zia   By . . . by the guys you must be, like. Fighting.

Gary   What?

Zia   Yeah.

Gary   Kidnapped, by Terry Taliban?

Zia *nods.*

Gary   That's what, that's what you're going with, is it?

Zia *nods.*

Zia   That's what happened, bruv.

Gary   Right. Well. Course. That all – actually – that all makes complete sense and you are now free to go.

He makes a mock gesture, presenting the doorway for **Zia** *to leave through.*

Gary   Sorry to have wasted your time and Paddy here will give you a reach-around and a kiss on the cheek for your trouble.

Hafizullah   What?

Gary   Is that what, is that what you want me to say?

Zia   Look . . .

Gary   Because I could, but it would just be words that I'd be throwing around the room like some kind of cunt chancer.

Zia   Look.

Gary   Wouldn't it?

Zia   I can understand – totally – if you don't like, believe that.

Gary   Big o' ya.

Zia   Cos I know it don't look good from where you're standing, from what you . . . from all what you're saying. But what I'm trying to do, is tell you. The truth.

Gary   Yeah?

Zia *nods.*

Zia   I'm . . . Yeah.

Gary   Well then, tell me the truth, bruv.

Zia   I'm trying to but you keep . . . fucking . . .

Gary   What?

Zia   Like. Interrupting.

Gary   Yeah?

Zia   Yes. It's quite. Annoying actually.

He nods.

Pause.

Gary *breaks into a smile, laughs a bit.*

Gary   Is it?

Zia *nods.*

Gary (*to* **Hafizullah**)   God, where are my manners today?
Eh?

He shakes his head.

Hafizullah   What?

Gary   Not allowing the gentleman to finish his story. OK
then. Alright. You have the fucking. Floor, Zia.

He nods. Gestures again.

Don't ya?

Pause.

Zia   OK. OK. Thank you. It just all got a bit. Much.

Gary   What did?

Zia   Holiday.

Gary   Back up.

Zia   What?

Gary   Back. Up. Where are we?

Zia   OK. OK. I was. I was with my uncle in Lahore, yeah?
For the holiday. Just like a family thing. Just visiting for a few
weeks, like on the break from college. And, and I was a bit . . .

Gary   Of a terrorist?

Zia   No. No. I was a bit lonely, to be honest with you. Not in a gay way. I just. Missed it.

Gary   What?

Zia   England. Home.

Gary   Yeah?

Zia   Yes.

Pause.

Gary   What about it?

Zia   Everything, bruv. Pakistan is so . . . like. Everything. Decent cars. Decent TV. Decent. Women. All of it, you know? Something to do. Anything. You don't realise till you go. What you. Miss.

Gary   Yeah?

Zia   Yeah. (*Pause.*) And my uncle's bit of a. Dick. Like he's a proper. Total. And my auntie, she *talks* like. *Constantly*. About. Nothing. I mean she could, she could talk to you for three hours non-stop about her *shoes* or something, I swear that. Like, I think she literally did that first day I got there. Just sat me down in the kitchen and talked and talked and talked and *then* showed me so many fucking photos you would not believe that. They've just got this like this digital camera thing – fuck me, yeah? – and they will take like a picture of every single family person in every single room in every single possible combination of all those people – you know what family are like, yeah? – and they will then show you every single one of them they take in order and talk you through the whole fucking thing and you have to visibly show that you are very interested by *all of them.*

Gary   Right.

Zia   And I musta seen like . . .

Gary   Fascinating.

Zia   And all this. So I was thinking about coming home early anyways, but then . . .

Gary   You joined the insurgency.

Zia   I thought . . . I thought you said you wouldn't like. Interrupt.

Gary *looks at him as if to say 'don't push your luck'.*

Gary   . . .

Zia   Anyway, moving on, yeah. Then. Then, after a few days of that, my uncle's . . . my uncle's friend. This business associate. He comes over to their house, visiting as part of his business, and he's this fucked-up, crazy Afghan guy, yeah?

Gary   Called?

Zia   Mohammed.

Gary   Original.

Zia   Mohammed Qasim.

Gary   Is it?

Zia *nods.*

Zia   And him and my uncle got this tidy little profit ting going on, yeah? Like he's bringing all these, like, all these textiles over from Kabul.

Gary   OK.

Zia   Yeah, and they're using them in my uncle's massive, like, factory in Lahore and making plenty of cash, bruv. And this guy, this guy, he's like – Mohammed Qasim – proper *crazy*. He's always laughing and joking and smiling and he's got this *energy*, you know, when he comes into the room and we get on *like this immediately* – fucking . . . sparks – he speaks well good English, which is great because my Urdu is a bit fucked up, a bit rusty to be honest with you, and I probably speak less Pashtu than you, yeah?

Gary   Is this going anywhere?

Zia What?

Gary Cos you're boring the arse off Paddy, for starters, mate.

Hafizullah What?

Gary Aren't ya?

Zia And he says to me. Mohammed Qasim says to me – I'm getting there, alright? OK? I'm getting there, soon, hold on, hold up, bruv – after we've been chatting bare shit for ages, he says: 'I like you. I like you, Zia, very much. We got a connection. So. You. Me. You, you come to Afghanistan with me. I'm going back for more supplies. I'll be two weeks at the most and you will see the most beautiful things and the most beautiful people in the whole world.'

Gary He said that?

Zia *nods.*

Zia And I was all like: 'Fuck that, yeah?' I was polite, though, I didn't actually swear when I actually said it – like he's a friend of the family, you know what I'm saying? – but I was all like: 'Thank you very much, that is a brilliant offer, thank you so much for that, but I can't do that, yeah? I would love to, yeah, but that is way too dangerous for me. There's a war there, you know what I'm saying? But he was all like: 'No no no, Zia, with me, with me you will be safe. There will be no problems with me. I know all the people, I am loved and known by all the people all around there and I will protect you. So if you say "No", you're disrespecting *me*, my family, my country and *my honour as a Muslim*.' (*Pause.*) So I'm like . . . Like: 'OK. Yeah. If . . . I will then. Thank you.' Even though I really didn't want to. And then.

Gary Zia.

Zia And then . . .

Gary *Zia.*

Zia – we . . . we . . . and *then* . . .

Gary   I think, I think I can see where this is going.

Zia   What?

Gary   And I reckon that's about enough.

Zia   But –

Gary   Now.

Zia   Na na na, but – listen – I'm not . . . finished. I'm not. *Started*.

Gary   Yeah you are. Done.

He nods.

Zia   . . .

Gary   Though, maybe we should phone a friend. Ask the audience. So what d'ya reckon then, Paddy?

Hafizullah   What?

Gary   You believe any o' this?

Hafizullah *shrugs.*

Gary   Fair enough, if you do. He's very like. Convincing. Inny?

Hafizullah   . . .

Gary   Got all the details right. Bit o' patter. Softening us up, all ready for the bit where Terry jumps him from nowhere, or whatever. Even doing the old patriotic bit.

Zia   No, that's not what . . .

Gary   But. He's got one tiny fucking problem.

Hafizullah   What?

Gary   Well, Paddy – nice of you to ask – in my class at school, there was only three white kids, including me. So all I heard, all day long, was exactly this kinda gangsta sing-song *bullshit*.

Zia Gangsta?

Gary And you get used to 'em – you do – denying *everything* under the fucking sun, even when everyone knows – you, them, the fucking . . . teachers – that, they done it. And I tell ya what, pretty quickly it starts to wear. Very. Fucking. Thin.

He gives **Zia** *a very pointed look.*

Zia Look. I'm not a . . . a 'gangsta'.

Gary *scoffs.*

Gary Semantics.

Zia And I'm not saying generally I'm like. Mother Teresa or . . . I done a little bit of fucked-up shit like everyone I know, yeah? Like I'm sure you done. But, I didn't try to *kill* no one. That is not . . . I'm not . . . I was . . . I was *kidnapped* and and I . . . I don't know how else to tell you this. I mean, do I look like a fucking . . . ?

Gary Yeah, yeah, you do 'n that.

Zia What? What you talking about? Everyone wears this.

Gary No.

Zia Um. Yeah.

Gary 'Um.' No.

Zia Yes.

Gary I don't.

Zia But . . . no, no, everyone *here*.

Gary *(referring to* **Hafizullah***)* He don't.

Zia Yeah, *yeah*, but . . .

Gary None of them lot do. I mean he's got a pair of fucking. Jeans. Fucking. Polo necks. Shirts. Normal. Eighties but normal. I seen 'em.

Zia Normal's not . . .

Gary   Don't ya?

Hafizullah *nods.*

Hafizullah   Yes.

Gary   See?

Zia   Look.

Gary   No.

Zia   But I'm . . . I'm in the middle here, mate. That is all
it is. I got caught up, bruv. Just, *trust me* on that. I swear to
you. I just wanna . . . I just wanna go home.

Gary   Yeah?

Zia   Yes.

Zia *nods.*

Gary *nods.*

A longish pause, during which **Gary** *looks outside, trying to collect his
thoughts. He then turns his attention back into the room.*

Gary   Where you from?

Zia   What?

Gary   Cos you sound London. Are you London? (*Pause.*)
What, you deaf as well as Asian?

Zia   No.

Gary   Well then. Are you London?

Pause.

Zia *nods.*

Gary   Thought so. Where?

Zia   . . .

Gary   . . . ?

Zia   East.

Gary   Yeah?

Zia *nods.*

Gary   Whereabouts?

Zia   Um.

Gary   Where?

Zia   Newham.

Gary   What?

Zia   Newham.

Gary   Fuck me.

Zia   Why . . . is that . . . ?

Gary   *Newham?*

Zia *nods.*

Gary   I got . . . I got cousins round there.

Zia   Yeah? Yeah, it's alright. Leafy.

Gary   No it ain't, it's a fucking . . . shit-heap. Where?

Zia   I said. Newham.

Gary   No, where *in* Newham? I know it, don't I? I got family and I'm from fucking. Tottenham.

Zia   Oh, right. That's. Close. Sort of.

Gary   *Yes, I know, that's why I'm fucking asking.* (*Pause.*) So?

Zia   Um, yeah. Wanstead Park.

Gary   Which bit?

Zia   Near the, the train station. Overground.

Gary   Oh for fuck . . .

Zia   . . . ? Why . . . is that . . .?

Gary   That's right . . . that's right by where my auntie is. Fucking . . . You think Wanstead Park is nice?

Zia   Um. Bits of it. Yeah. No, not really though, no, obviously. Fucking, rubbish.

Gary   Whatever he is, I think we've picked up a fucking . . . loon here, Paddy.

Hafizullah   What?

Gary *nods.*

Gary   Yeah, fucking . . . headcase, he likes Wanstead Park. (*Pause.*) So you're a Hammer then?

Zia   . . . ? What?

Gary   You are a Hammer then.

Zia   I don't know what, what you're . . . ?

Gary   The football team. West Ham. If you're from down there.

Zia   Oh. Yeah. Um . . . No. No, I don't . . .

Gary   Who then?

Zia   No, I mean I don't really follow any . . .

Gary   Yeah you do.

Zia   OK. Erm. If I had to.

Gary   Yes. You do.

Zia   OK then. Erm. Liverpool.

Gary   What?

Zia   My brother took me when I was a kid – Anfield – so . . .

Gary   I was glassed by a Scouser once. At a wedding. He was Everton but.

Zia   Yeah, I don't support 'em any more though, yeah? I'm just saying that cos you asked me. If I had to. So . . . so . . . what about . . . what about . . . you?

Gary   What?

Zia Who do you like . . . support?

Gary Tottenham.

Zia Yeah?

Gary *nods.*

Gary Yeah. Funny that.

Zia Yeah, they're . . . they're good. Good team. Sleeping. Like. Giant.

Gary *nods.*

Zia With. Gary Lineker.

Gary *nods.*

Zia *nods.*

Zia Gary. Mabbutt. He had. Erm. Diabetes.

Gary Yes. He did. He does. You're a proper fucking expert, aren't ya? You should write a fucking book.

Zia *shrugs ironically/desperately.*

Pause.

Zia Look. I really . . . I really didn't come here to, to hurt you. That's not what I'm about, yeah? And you seem like a, a good guy and and I want you to know that – right? – I want you to know that.

Gary Right.

Zia I do.

Zia *nods.*

Gary *nods.*

Pause.

Gary Guess who he supports.

Zia What?

Gary Guess which football team Paddy there supports.

Zia   I . . . I don't know.

Gary   Believe me, guess and you'll get it.

Zia   Erm . . .

Gary   First time.

Zia *considers.*

Zia   Er . . .

Gary   Come on.

Zia   Alright.

Gary   You'll kick yourself.

Zia   OK.

Gary   Cos you do, ya know it.

Pause.

Zia   Is it. Manchester United?

Gary   Yep.

Hafizullah   Yes.

Zia   Right.

Gary   Only thing he wants to talk about some days. I'm actually properly sick of it.

Zia *nods. Tries a smile.*

Zia   Yeah.

Gary   Yeah, and rather than wasting your breath lying to me – begging – you should probably just have a chat with him about. Gary Neville. Or. Paul Scholes.

He nods.

Zia   OK, that's . . .

Gary   While you still can.

Pause.

Zia   What . . . ? What d'ya mean?

Gary   Well. 'Look.'

Zia   . . . ?

Gary   Put it this way. Where you're going – soon – you'll be wishing you was in an orange jumpsuit out in Cuba somewhere.

Zia   I don't . . . You're talking about football and then you're . . . I don't get what. Jumpsuit? I'm on holiday. I'm, I'm on . . . and things just got a bit fucked up, yeah? That's all it is. That is all it is, I keep telling you that.

Gary   Course.

Zia   So what . . . ? What are you gonna . . . do, to me?

Gary   Me? Fuck all, mate. Nothing. I mean, we'll get the medic in here, see you over, when he's done with . . . as soon as he's done out there. And he'll sort you out. Patch up your leg, splint, little bandage, clean up the wound. Even make sure you're hydrated. All very civilised, actually. But then.

Zia   . . . ? Then . . . ?

Gary   Then, we hand you over.

Zia   To . . . ?

Gary   (*referring to* **Hafizullah**)   His lot. ANA. Afghan Army, the fuckers we're training here, bruv. And, believe it or not, they ain't all like him. Lot of 'em are, but some. Some of them. *Well.*

Zia   This ain't . . .

Gary   Tell you a funny story, shall I?

Zia   . . . ?

Gary *nods.*

Pause.

Gary   Last week. Last Sunday. I'm going into their compound with Phippy, my . . . my mate. And the ANA have got one. One of your lot, they got a prisoner on the ground, just outside their guardroom. And they're. Hitting him. (*He nods.*) With the end of a pistol, which they're – two of 'em – taking it in turns to use. (*Pause.*) And I seen some proper beatings, beastings, millings, before. Bad ones. And usually they stop. Pretty quick. When someone like steps in, or, they ease off, run out of steam, whatever. But na. They was just like:

He intimates the level of sustained and prolonged force with a small, measured gesture, repeated twice.

We pulled the snatch wagon up and we just. Me and Phippy, we just. Sat there, watched 'em. And for about ten minutes, they kept going. His face was like . . . Each impact. And the thing was, the blokes, the ANA guys doing it. They weren't even that, like, worked up, angry, or. One of 'em – right? – one of 'em, clocked me, watching him. And he stopped for a second. Turned round. Looked at me.

He nods a little.

And, he was grinning like a little fucking kid. Except he had blood all up his face. And he. Smiled. Nodded. Grinned. And then. Then he just, turned back, wiped the blood off his hand and just. Carried on. (*He nods. Pause.*) Then a fucking crowd gathered and things got *really nasty*, if you know what I mean. So, we left 'em to it. Fucking . . . And this – clearly – to them. Like. Spectator sport. Bit o' fun. Out here, that's how it goes. And I'll be very fucking surprised if you have a nicer way out, to be honest. You didn't kill any of my lot but the ANA, they lost three guys today in the main contact, so – apart from Paddy here, obviously – they're proper wound up. Tight as you like.

Zia   But I ain't done nothing to them.

Gary   Yeah, they might not see it like that.

Zia   But . . .

Gary   We already had one in here, sizing you up.

He breaks into a smile.

Zia Na, man. Look. *Look.* What do you want me to . . . to say to you? I can answer any question you got. Any. Any one. You, you ask me. Come on, yeah? *Please.* (*Pause.*) Anything.

No response.

Look, I'm British, yeah? I got. I got rights. I know that, bruv. *I know that.* And you can't do that. You can't *let them* do that. I am. British.

Gary Yeah, what, do you want, a medal?

Zia Legally, I'm . . .

Gary Son. Soon as you fire at someone. Me, my mates, I reckon you lose that kind of right. Don't care where you're from.

Zia But I'm . . . I am . . .

Hafizullah He is. Very.

Gary *and* **Zia** *look at* **Hafizullah**.

Gary What?

Hafizullah Scared.

Gary Well . . . well, yeah, he should be, Paddy.

Hafizullah (*nodding*) Yes.

Pause.

Gary What about it?

Having finished his previous joint, **Hafizullah** *has made another. He considers it for a moment before moving forward on his knees and offering it to* **Zia**.

Zia Wha's he doing?

Gary He's . . . Jesus Christ.

Zia What?

Gary *exhales.*

Gary   Tit that he is, Paddy is. Offering you a toke.

Zia   Wh . . . why?

Gary   Because. Because he thinks you might need one.

He shakes his head.

Zia   So, what? What do I do?

Gary   Whatever.

Zia   But . . .

Gary   Look. 'Look.' It ain't a trick or nothing. He ain't like that. He's just offering you some green, that's all. They all smoke 'em. Their guardhouse is like a fucking crack den in Brixton or somewhere. If you don't want it: don't. If you do: do.

Zia *thinks about this for a second and then nods, a little unsurely, to* **Hafizullah***.*

Zia   OK.

Hafizullah *nods, lights the joint and hands it to* **Zia***.*

While this is happening, **Gary** *takes a quick look outside. Coming back into the room, he watches* **Zia** *take a tentative drag.*

Zia *lets out a deep breath/cloud of smoke. Coughs.*

Gary   How is it?

Zia   Strong.

Gary *nods.*

Zia *coughs.*

Zia   Fuck.

Gary   Yeah, will be. Fresh.

Zia *nods and takes another drag. Exhales. Stifles a cough.*

Gary   Might even have some opium in it. If you're lucky.

Zia   What?

Gary   For your leg. Pain.

Zia *nods.*

Zia OK. (*A longish pause.*) I ain't lying.

He coughs a bit.

Gary Don't. Don't start, alright? Enjoy your spliff, cough it up, but – please – shut the fuck up.

Zia . . .

Pause.

He takes another drag and then offers **Gary** *the joint.*

Gary *shakes his head.*

Zia *offers it back to* **Hafizullah**, *who comes over and takes it from him.*

Zia Thank you.

Hafizullah *nods and then goes back to his corner.*

Zia Please. I was just visiting my uncle.

Gary Chief. Before you start – again – I'm gonna tell you something. Gratis.

Zia . . . ?

Gary Save your breath. We ain't got no facilities yet for prisoners or nothing like that, we just got here. Our FOB is pretty much made out of cardboard so far. You could fart your way out of detention if we had to build you a cell or whatever. So. Even if we wanted to – which we don't – we can't take ya. That's the bottom line. But – right? – much more importantly: I'm not gonna believe anything you say. Cos I know your innit-bruv type enough to know the only time you ain't lying is when you ain't talking. So, I won't listen to ya, and the ANA, they *definitely* won't.

Zia But . . .

Gary So. This is how it goes: I'm a soldier, you're a soldier. (*Referring to* **Hafizullah**.) Even he is, technically. And these things happen when you decide to fight. Yeah? So shut up, save all your lies for the big man upstairs, accept what's gonna happen to ya and make your peace. You understand that? Best way.

Zia   You can't . . . do this.

Gary   Watch me.

Zia   But I'm. British.

Gary   So am I. Ain't it marvellous?

Zia   Please, I'm . . .

Gary   Shut. Fuck. Up.

A long pause, after which **Simon** *appears in the doorway.*

Simon   Can I . . . ? I need a word.

Gary   You ain't gonna believe this one, sir.

Simon   Outside.

Gary *looks at* **Simon** *and clocks that this is something serious.*

He nods.

Gary   OK.

Simon (*gesturing to* **Hafizullah**)   And you're sure it's alright leaving him in here with . . . ?

Gary   Honestly, not a problem.

Simon   Well then.

He gestures with his head for **Gary** *to follow him outside.*

He exits.

As **Gary** *goes towards the doorway, he glances back at* **Zia**.

Gary   Eyes-on, Paddy.

He does a two-fingered 'eyes-on' gesture.

Hafizullah *nods.*

Gary   Good lad.

He exits.

A longish pause.

Zia   *A salaam alaikum.*

No reponse.

I take it Paddy ain't your real name?

Hafizullah *shakes his head.*

Zia   Na. So what is?

No response.

What is it?

No response.

Look. These. These, are hurting me. Would you . . . ? Would you help me? With a like a knife or something?

He gestures with his plasticuffs, wanting them cut.

No response.

Think they're cutting off blood.

No response.

Look. Paddy, whatever. I could. I could pay you.

Hafizullah *looks up at* **Zia**.

Zia   My father is. Quite rich. My family. He's a doctor. GP. Could set you up. For life.

Hafizullah   What?

Zia   Proper money. Believe that.

Hafizullah   I don't want . . . your . . .

Zia   OK. OK. So what . . . ? What do you want?

Hafizullah   To sleep.

Pause.

Zia   They're gonna . . . they're gonna kill me and I'm . . . I'm not . . . Can't you see that? That, I'm innocent of this?

Hafizullah *shrugs.*

Zia *exhales.*

Zia   . . .

He shakes his head a little bit.

Pause.

How old are you?

Hafizullah   Nineteen.

Zia   Yeah?

Hafizullah *nods.*

Zia   You look. Older.

Hafizullah *shrugs.*

Zia   I'm twenty-two. Too young for this.

Hafizullah   No age is good.

Zia   No, but. Look. I'm. I'm begging you. Anything that you want, I can get you. I'm like that. I am good to know. Even here. Even now.

Hafizullah *looks down, away from* **Zia**'s *stare.*

Zia   No, look at me. No – like he told you – look at me.

Hafizullah *eventually looks up.*

Zia   We're. Brothers. Ain't we? *Inshaallah.*

Hafizullah *looks down again.*

Zia   No no, stay. Stay with me. Listen. Listen to what I'm saying.

Hafizullah   Why?

Zia   Because. Because I want you to understand this, what they're doing to me.

Hafizullah I do.

Zia *shakes his head.*

Zia No. No. You don't.

Hafizullah *looks up.*

Zia Look.

Zia *holds* **Hafizullah**'s *gaze.*

Hafizullah I know.

Zia No. You don't. Listen to me.

Enter **Gary**. *He looks fiercely at* **Zia**, *standing over him.*

Zia . . . ?

Gary *keeps looking at him.*

Gary (*in shock; to himself, if anyone*) Fuck.

Zia What?

Gary *Fuck.*

Zia What?

Gary Zia.

Zia . . . ?

Gary You better make a wish.

Zia What did I do?

Gary Won't need a pistol, way I'm gonna do it.

Zia . . . ?

Gary *nods.*

Gary Yeah.

Enter **Simon**.

Simon Are you sure that you're . . . ? That you . . . ?

Gary Yes, sir, I told ya, I'm . . .

Simon   Because . . .

Gary *looks at* **Simon** *over his shoulder.*

Simon   I don't want you – or any of the others – taking it out on . . . We leave all that to the bloody . . . savages. Alright?

Gary *nods.*

Simon   Is that understood?

Gary   Crystal.

Simon   OK. OK.

Gary   I'll be fine with him, sir, honestly. Kid gloves.

Simon   Right. (*Pause.*) I see he's . . . he's up now.

Gary *nods.*

Simon   Quite. Tubby. Isn't he? For a Terry.

Gary   Yeah.

Pause.

Simon   I don't like the way he's looking at me. Sort of. Feral. God, look at him. Has he been talking?

Gary *shrugs.*

Gary   . . .

Simon   Anything other than '*Allahu Akbar*'?

Gary   Not really.

Simon   So what, has Bob Marley here been translating?

Hafizullah   What?

Gary   Yeah.

Simon   Then what's his story?

Zia   I'm actually, on holiday.

Simon   . . . ?

Zia *nods.*

Zia   Yeah and I can, I can explain it all to you. Just, just give me five minutes of your day.

Awkwardly (because of the cuffs) he holds up five fingers to emphasise the point.

Simon   You're . . . ?

Zia *tries to smile.*

Zia   Yeah. Hello.

He offers the 'five' hand, offering **Simon** *to shake it.*

Pause.

Simon   And you . . . you didn't care to mention that?

Gary   Yeah, sorry, sir. I was gonna but I got a bit . . . distracted. Can't think why.

Simon   But he's . . . isn't he?

Gary   I don't give a fuck if he's . . . Polish. Phippy is out there, *fucking* . . .

Simon   I know.

Gary   I feel like. *Sick.*

Simon   Just. Come on. Breathe.

Gary   Breathe? Fucking . . . *breathe*? That's your advice, is it?

Simon   OK. OK. Today – yes – today has been . . .

Gary   What? What has it, sir?

Simon   A lot. Hot. Long. But you're not . . . you're not helping yourself. Anyone.

Gary   Who are you, Jeremy Kyle?

Simon   Now you're being pretty fucking *tedious* here, actually.

Gary   Oh, I'm sorry, sir, I'm just . . . I've just heard that my . . . fucking . . .

Simon   Yes. You have. And I've just watched him . . . so don't . . . Harris. Matters at hand. OK?

Gary *shrugs/scoffs.*

Simon   *OK?*

Pause.

Gary *nods.*

Gary   Yeah.

Simon   Good. Right. So what's he been saying?

Gary   I dunno. Some . . .

Simon   What?

Gary   . . . butter-wouldn't-melt. Bullshit.

Zia   It ain't bullshit.

Gary   Course not.

Simon   Like what?

Gary   Nothing . . . worth repeating, sir.

Zia   *No no,* I was, I was *kidnapped.*

Gary   *Oh, will you shut your cunt mouth, before I fucking* . . .

Simon   No, you weren't. We found you.

Zia   No no, by them.

Simon   Who?

Zia   The . . .

Gary   *Taliban.* He reckons he's . . . he reckons he's some fucking . . .

Simon   Reckons . . . ?

Gary   I dunno, this . . . Some . . .

Simon   . . . ?

Gary   Sir. Sir. He started. He started coming out with all this . . . this . . . But I didn't really see the point in listening to some . . . bullshit fucking . . . He's just . . . he's just made up. He's a Terry. He's been caught.

Simon Right.

Gary Simple.

Simon Yeah.

Gary So he's made up some. Story.

Simon OK.

Gary Case closed.

Simon Well, let's not . . .

Gary Innit?

Simon Corporal.

Gary Ain't it, sir?

Pause.

Simon So how does he claim they got him?

Gary Irrelevant.

Simon It might not be, that's what I'm saying.

Gary Course it is. Obvious.

Simon Look. We're almost definitely facing a long wait. And if we have some information here, on this situation, on what happened to Phipps this morning – all of it – then I'd like to obtain that. Now. Rather than swear at him and kick our feet in the sand like children. Is that crystal?

Gary Sir.

Simon Is it?

Pause.

Gary . . .

He shrugs.

Simon Good. I'm glad you. So what have we got, so far?

Pause.

Gary *sighs.*

Gary   He's from London. Newham. Called. Zia.

Zia   Z-I-A. Starts with a 'Z', rhymes with . . .

Gary   Yeah. Zia.

Simon   A youth from London. No wonder he was armed.

Gary   Reckons he was visiting. Like. Family.

Zia   I was. In Lahore.

Simon   OK. And then what? How's he get here?

Gary   Well, he says . . .

Zia   Whoa whoa whoa, can I not like, talk for myself?

Gary   I think you said your piece with the RPG, mate.

Zia (*to* **Gary**)   Are you in charge?

Gary   What?

Zia   I said: are you in charge here?

Gary   What the . . . ?

Zia   Exactly. He is. (*To* **Simon**.) And I think – all things –
that you want to hear it from me. Am I right, though?

Simon   Two things. Firstly, yes, yes, I am in charge, lucky old
me. Secondly, if you talk like that to us – either of us – again,
you'll either regret it or you won't remember regretting it.

Zia   . . .

Simon   OK?

Zia   Yeah. Yeah. OK. Of course.

He nods.

Gary   I thought we weren't meant to hurt him, sir.

Simon   I have special privileges, Lance Corporal: I am the
Lord of Death. Right. So where are we?

Gary   Then. Then he was talking for fucking ages about he got pissed off with his family he was visiting in . . .

Zia   Lahore.

Gary   Lahore, and then, then he decides to . . . to come here with some business cunt.

Zia   Mohammed Qasim. He was alright.

Simon   Why?

Zia   What?

Simon   Why come here?

Zia   Cos I was invited and it was business and he told me it would be safe and . . . I don't . . . because . . .

Simon   Because . . . ?

Zia   Cos I always, like . . . sort o' . . .

Simon   . . . ?

Zia   . . . wanted to.

Simon   What?

Zia   I mean. Like. Sometimes. Like. You hear from people back home that, out here, it's meant to be like: pure. Like, how it was back in the day, before we got: money money money, me me me, yeah? And I wanted to see that. For myself. While I could.

Simon   Really? That's what people say? Back home?

Zia *nods.*

Gary   No, they don't.

Zia *nods.*

Simon   Because – from my own perspective – having spent the majority of my adult life in Richmond and now being able to compare the two – for what it's worth – I very much think that I prefer money money money, me me me, actually. Given the choice.

Zia   Me too, now. That's what I'm saying, that's why I wanna just get back. Home. Like I told you. Him. Yeah, you're right. You are.

Pause.

Simon   So what, did you fly here? Drive? Crawl?

Zia   Drive, yeah. In a lorry truck thing.

Simon   From . . . ?

Zia   From Quetta to Kandahar, then, then west.

Simon   Long drive. You drove from Lahore to Quetta, to start with?

Zia   Yeah, but it was a like a, a, a business route and it's his decision and business is business so who am I to, like . . . ? And it is – you're right – a long, long drive, yeah? But, that way I get to see more of the country, meet more of the, the *people*, so I'm like, 'Hey, no problem for me, this. No. No problem.'

Simon   Right.

Zia   Wind in my hair. Arm on the door, window down. Him telling me stories all day. Good times.

Simon   Yeah, sounds amazing. So what the fuck happens next?

Zia   We . . . like . . . yeah, we pull into this little town, Musa Qala, which is where this market is we're going to pick up these, these goods.

Gary (*to* **Simon**)   That market. That's where Davey Thomas got . . .

Simon *nods.*

Simon   Yeah.

Zia   And then – you know it – in the middle of there, the market, along the main road, is all . . . all these like men wearing the shalwar kameez and all that, like normal but all these, these guys, their clothes are, are all: black. All over. And Mohammed Qasim.

Gary   The cunt who don't exist.

Zia   Yeah. No. Mohammed Qasim says to me, that ain't normal. This. This ain't normal. This town is usually like . . .

Simon   Friendly.

Zia   Yeah, but these guys, the way they're walking, moving, they're like outsiders or something and something messed up is going on and before we know it, they're looking at us. Coming at us. Surrounding us, and they got all these guns, which they're holding up like . . . (*Pause.*) And they make him. Mohammed Qasim. Step out the vehicle. They walk him round in front of where we was parked. He has to . . . to kneel down. They make him. Kneel down in front of them. On the floor. The road. And they, like they . . . (*Pause.*) They shoot him. Through the, through the face and it's . . . the back of his head is like . . . Then, then they pull me out the truck and I'm . . . I don't mind admitting this to you, yeah? – I'm *begging* them. Crying. 'Show me mercy.' I'm a Muslim like them, yeah? All this. *Anything*. To, *save* myself. But they're just, laughing at me. Laughing. They've taken all my . . . my possessions – passport, money, *everything* – and they are emptying them all over the ground in front of me, from my bag. And I think: '*Fuck*. I am going to die. Here. Now. This, this is the end of my life.' (*Pause.*) And I feel like I'm gonna burst or something. And it all goes. Quiet. Like, in a film or something. And all I want is. Mercy. You know? But I must still be talking and screaming cos through it I can tell, that they've heard me and they must recognise my, my accent, that I'm: *British*. Or maybe they got it from my, my, my passport, I don't know, but I hear them say: 'British.' I don't understand the other words or none of that yeah but . . . I hear that: 'British. British.' And then they start. Talking. For ages.

Zia *nods.*

Gary *shakes his head.*

Gary   Fuck me. You got some stones. Gi' ya that.

Simon   And then what?

Zia   Then, then they musta worked out that I'm worth more to them like. Alive.

Gary   . . . ?

Zia   Yeah, for the ransom.

Gary   What?

Zia   Happens all the time in Pakistan, yeah? Cos in the UK we're like Bill Gates or something to these people, so they kidnap like, like a relative, yeah, and then they make the person in England or whatever pay for them to get out.

Gary   Paddy, Paddy, does that happen?

Hafizullah *nods.*

Hafizullah   Yes.

Zia   *Exactly.* Even your mate says so and they must think they can get hold of my family, get this money, the money from them, yeah? Which would then, would make them rich. Beyond anything they got here. (*To* **Hafizullah**.) Ain't that right though?

Hafizullah *nods.*

Gary   Paddy.

Zia   And so, so they they take me to this building like this, a room like this, and they kept me there. They fed me, didn't hurt me or nothing, and I'm thinking, I'm thinking – fuck – they're working out a way to contact my family or something, using my passport and my address book. Which they got now. And that was like two weeks they kept me there in this one little room. Like this. Just. Waiting. They didn't tell me. Nothing.

Pause.

Simon   We didn't find you in any room.

Zia No, no, but today – today – everything starts. The noise was like. Explosions everywhere and this big guy comes in, one o' them I ain't seen before, and he comes in and puts me on his *shoulder* and takes me outside. And. As we're like, running, going outside, get near to, to these trees – like an orchard or something – in front of us but. Before we get there. This force hits us and we're going back through the air and everything and . . . and yeah, then I land on my leg, remember that. Think I must black out with the *pain* or something. And then . . .

Simon Then . . . ?

Zia Then. I wake up. Here.

He nods.

Yeah.

Pause.

Gary Are you done?

Zia *nods.*

Gary Good, cos so am I now. (*Scoffs. To* **Simon**.) Told ya.

Simon You do know we can check all this out? About the factory. Everything.

Zia *nods.*

Gary . . . ?

Simon What about the Kalashnikov?

Gary Why . . . ? Why are you even . . . ?

Zia Maybe, maybe that belonged to the big guy, I don't know. I don't remember, I was *out*. I swear to you.

Gary The big guy that we *didn't find*. Funny that.

Hafizullah Maybe Taliban. Take him.

Gary . . . ?

They look to **Hafizullah**.

Hafizullah   Taliban never leave fighter.

Zia   Yeah, I heard that.

Hafizullah   Bad for honour, you find body.

Gary   But leave his AK?

Hafizullah *shrugs.*

Hafizullah   I don't know.

Gary   Na, na, you don't, mate. So shut the fuck up.

Hafizullah   But maybe he . . .

Gary   *Paddy.* Leave it to the *adults.* Alright?

Hafizullah *looks to* **Gary**.

Gary   And don't . . . don't look at me like that, fuck sake.

He looks away.

Hafizullah   . . .

Gary   You're not . . . you're not actually buying this, are you, sir? All this?

Simon   Doesn't really matter what I think.

Gary   Yeah. Yeah, suppose not. ANA won't care.

Simon   What?

Gary   They won't give a fuck. Just carve him up, be done with it.

Simon   You don't still think that we're . . . handing him over?

Gary   Why not? We did with the last one and with him you said, you *ordered me* ta fucking . . .

Simon   The last one was a gap-toothed mujahedin, some . . . . local.

Gary   And what's he a, Liberal Democrat?

Simon   No, no, he's fucking . . . *English.*

Zia (*nodding*)   British.

Gary   So what? Being *English* isn't helping Phippy out there, is it? Fucking . . . is it? So why . . . with him . . . is it now all of a sudden some fucking . . . ?

Simon   Corporal. This kid is entitled, like it or not, to consular access. So someone – somewhere – some wonky civil servant will have to come out from behind their paper clips and make representation on his behalf. And if they do, and find that all the ANA have got left is a . . . an *ear* on a fucking *key ring,* they might possibly think something's gone wrong somewhere. Can you not see that? Can you not see how this would play out, for us?

Gary *scoffs.*

Gary   But who needs to fucking know, sir? Not like ANA are gonna check his papers first, fill out any fucking . . . forms or nothing. Doubt he'll get much of a chance to *speak* let alone . . . So, who the fuck, is gonna find out?

Simon   . . .

Gary   Paddy won't tell no one. You think I will? And, and, where we gonna put him? The FOB's barely got enough beds for us, sir – let alone some fucking – and having him on the inside of that wall is, is – all due respect, sir – fucking *madness.* Just let the ANA take him wherever the fuck they take 'em.

Simon   He'll be going on the casevac. Back to Bastion.

Gary   What? With Phippy?

Simon   Yeah.

Gary   But . . . ? What if he . . . what if he does something? In the air?

Simon   He'll be tied up. What can he do? Will the thing to crash?

Gary   Great. Oh, *great.* You do realise he might have been – probably was – the cunt who fired the RPG? You get that? And you're gonna put him next to his . . . ?

Simon   Corporal. I know you're upset. But you're gabbling, that's all you're doing.

Gary   Sir. *Sir.*

Simon   *What?*

Gary   *Honestly this is fucking* . . .

Simon   No. No. You need to calm the fuck down and listen to me, before I run out of TLC.

Gary   Do I have to, sir?

Simon   If he's guilty, then we're gonna wanna know how he got here. If he's not, we can't let him burn. Either way.

Gary *shakes his head.*

Zia   . . .

Gary *points at* **Zia** *as if to say, 'You dare say anything.'*

Gary   Na.

A pause, before:

From outside in the distance: 'Sir! Sir!'

Simon *sighs.*

Simon   Christ.

He tentatively goes to the doorway, looks out. Cries of 'Sir!'

Something is . . .

Cries of 'Sir!'

Pause.

(*To the soldiers outside.*) Yes. (*Turning back to* **Gary**.) Nothing happens to him. You understand that?

Gary   . . .

Simon   Do you understand?

Gary   Sir.

Simon   I'll be . . . hopefully, I won't be . . . *Do you understand?*

Gary *nods.*

Gary   Yes, sir.

Simon   You have to.

Gary *nods.*

Simon   Thank you.

He looks at **Gary**, *sighs.*

Simon   . . .

He exits, shaking his head slightly.

Gary *moves towards the doorway and watches* **Simon** *walking away.*

Pause.

Gary (*still looking outside*)   Zia. With a 'Z'. Do you wanna try and have a guess, why he called me out? Before?

Zia   I. Don't know.

Gary   Go on, have a fucking guess.

Zia   . . .

He shrugs.

Gary   Well. When the RPG – first one – came in today – from your position – it caught. Phippy. (*Pause.*) But I thought he was alright. I mean, he was laughing, joking after. He was. Taking the piss out of me for looking worried. So I just thought: bit o' shrapnel, he'll be right. (*He shakes his head.*) But. We been waiting so long. There's been contact today all over. Kajaki. Sangin. And there's only one Chinook, so he's . . . he's lost a lot of blood. A lot. Waiting. That's what he told me, just now. Knows we're close. (*Pause.*) So, you can tell by the way they called out for him, just now. Phippy will have . . . I think he's . . .

Pause.

Zia   I'm sorry to . . . about that.

Gary   And I have to say, that was a good story. A good account. I mean, did you have that all ready, worked out in advance, or was ya making it up as you went along?

Zia   . . .

Gary   Either way. Impressive. You had Rupert there . . . (*Gesturing to where* **Simon** *went.*) He thinks you're fucking. Terry Waite. (*Pause.*) But I do wonder. I do. If you could keep it up. Under pressure. Or would you crack, d'ya think?

Zia   What? I don't . . . I don't know what . . .

Gary *walks towards* **Zia**, *stands on the thigh of the broken leg and lifts his foot in the air, pushing his whole weight down in one forceful movement.*

Zia *screams; we hear a crack.*

Zia   *Fuck.*

Gary *moves away from* **Zia**.

Zia   *Fuck.* Ah . . .

He is breathing very heavily and gags through the sheer weight of pain/ panic.

Gary   Sorry, did that, did that hurt? I didn't hurt you, did I? Fucking shame that. (*He sniffs.*) How d'you get here?

Zia's *breathing starts to slow a little but is still loud and heavy.*

Gary   Tell me. Tell me or I do it again. (*Pause.*) Do you hear me, son? Because I will. Again and a-fucking-gain till you *do*.

Zia   I didn't . . . I didn't . . . I never done *nothing* to you.

Gary   Well, let's make sure o' that, shall we?

Gary *moves back towards* **Zia**.

Zia *tenses up in anticipation.*

Hafizullah   Gary. (*Reaching out.*) Gary.

Gary   What?

Hafizullah No.

Gary No what?

Hafizullah This.

Gary What are you . . . ?

Zia Fuck . . .

Gary What . . . what you talking about?

Hafizullah This.

Gary *This what?*

Zia Fuck . . .

Gary (*to* **Zia**) Shut up. What are you talking about, Paddy?

Hafizullah His leg. This. No.

Gary What . . . wha's it gotta do with you?

Hafizullah Nothing.

Gary *Exactly.* And it's 'nothing', like, like what your mates – ANA – they do. Is it? All the fucking time. You ever stop them?

Hafizullah *shrugs.*

Hafizullah . . .

Gary Then why you give a fuck?

Hafizullah I don't . . . I don't like to watch this.

Gary Then . . . then get out. If you don't wanna watch, Paddy, get out.

Hafizullah No.

Gary Then . . . then . . . fucking . . .

Hafizullah Taliban, make you watch.

Gary . . . ?

Hafizullah Taliban.

Gary . . . ?

Hafizullah They come into town. Village. Like this. Everyone, must watch. Like this.

Gary So . . . so what? Who cares?

Hafizullah Gary.

Gary *What?*

Pause.

Hafizullah I lose family, like this. My mother. Like this. I watch. (*Pause.*) Please.

Gary Fucking . . .

Hafizullah Please. Me.

Gary I'm not . . .

Hafizullah You. I know.

Gary I'm . . . I'm not . . .

Hafizullah Yes. I know.

Gary Fucking . . .

Hafizullah Yes.

A longish pause before **Gary** *goes and leans against the corner of the room opposite* **Zia** *and exhales loudly as he does so. After a while he turns and sits, sliding down the wall.*

A long pause.

Gary This day.

Hafizullah Yes.

Pause.

Zia Yeah.

Gary *and* **Zia** *briefly make eye contact.*

Gary Fuck.

A very long pause.

Who they play?

Pause.

Zia   Me?

Gary   Yeah. Who they play?

Zia   Who?

Gary   Liverpool. Anfield.

Zia   Erm.

He smiles a little, remembering.

You won't believe me.

Gary   Go on.

Hafizullah   Yes.

Zia   Erm . . .

He exhales.

Man U.

Gary   No.

Hafizullah   Yes?

Zia *nods.*

Gary *smiles a little and then nods.*

Pause.

Gary   Who. Who won?

Zia   It was a draw. Two all.

Gary   Right. (*Pause.*) Who scored?

Zia   Erm. Paul Ince got the equaliser. Last minute. The others . . .

He shrugs.

Gary *nods.*

Pause.

Gary   Who for?

Zia   What?

Gary   He played for both. Paul Ince.

Zia   Oh, yeah. Erm. Liverpool.

Gary   Right. Is that when. When Denis Irwin got sent off, for kicking the ball away?

Zia   That's right.

Gary   Yeah.

Zia   You remember that?

Gary   Yeah. I'm a bit. *Rain Man*, on that kinda stuff.

He nods.

Pause.

Holiday?

Zia *nods.*

Gary   Hope you got insurance.

Zia   From Boots. Online.

Gary *nods, forces a slight smile.*

Gary   Seriously. You came here to fight.

Zia   I'm . . .

Gary   Didn't ya?

Zia   I was in Lahore.

Gary   Course you were.

Zia   I was visiting my uncle and . . .

Gary   Yeah, yeah, yeah. Don't. How's your leg?

Zia   Fucked. How's your foot?

Gary   Not bad.

Zia and **Gary** *both nod a little.*

Gary   You'll like Bastion. Main base, so full o' people like me.

Zia   Great.

Gary   Thousands of 'em.

Zia   Can't wait.

Gary   Out in the desert.

A long pause during which **Gary** *sees the white plastic gloves in the dirt betweens his legs, picks them out, turns them over in his hand and then lets them drop back on the floor. Picks dirt up in his hand, pours it over them, burying them.*

Enter **Simon***.*

Pause.

Gary   Is he . . . ?

Simon   Phipps.

Gary   Yeah, is he . . . ?

Simon *nods.*

Simon   T4.

Gary   Right.

Pause.

Simon   I think – all told – it was a pretty quiet way to go. In the end.

Gary   Quiet?

Simon   As peaceful as you could. He slipped out of consciousness, and. That was that.

Gary   Yeah, I can't think of a nicer way to go than having my neck torn open by RPG shrapnel. Hope my nan goes like that.

A long pause.

Can I see him?

Simon   What?

Gary   I'd like to see him, sir.

Simon   If you think that's . . .

Gary *nods.*

Simon   . . .

Gary   We always said that. Whoever didn't . . . should like, shake the hand of the other. After. To see 'em off, into the . . . If we got the chance. A final.

Simon   OK.

Gary   Like, goodbye. Yeah, it was a promise, so.

Simon   OK, I'll stay here and . . . Of course.

Gary   Proper English send-off. Though he was Geordie, so he don't really count.

He nods a little.

He clambers to his feet, brushes himself off. Moves towards the doorway. Stops and looks at **Zia***.*

Gary   Watch him, Paddy. I mean it.

Hafizullah   OK.

Gary   . . .

He nods a little and holds **Hafizullah***'s look.* **Gary** *then takes one last look at* **Zia***, shakes his head and exits.*

After **Gary** *has gone,* **Simon** *moves into the doorway and watches him go. He takes a brief look back into the room at* **Hafizullah** *and* **Zia** *before turning away, leaning against the doorway, facing out, and taking out/lighting a cigarette from a packet of Marlboro Reds.*

A pause as he smokes, during which **Simon** *briefly looks back into the room again. Rubs his head, his exhaustion from the day starting to kick in.*

Zia *winces, getting more shooting pain from his leg.* **Hafizullah** *watches this.*

Zia   Ah . . .

Hafizullah (*gesturing to his drugs tin*)   You want, more?

Zia   Erm. Er . . .

He gets more shooting pain.

Hafizullah   . . . ?

Zia *nods.*

Hafizullah *nods and starts to make a smallish joint for* **Zia**.

Zia (*to* **Simon**)   Hey, do you mind if I . . . ?

Simon *looks round.*

Zia *gestures that he wants to smoke a joint.*

Zia   Do you mind if I . . . like, with him? For medicinal, whatever. My leg.

Simon *gestures along the lines of 'Do what you like, I don't care', and turns back facing out.*

Zia (*to* **Hafizullah**)   Think that's a yes.

Hafizullah *smiles a little, nods.*

Zia *watches him.*

Zia   Like the way you guys don't put no tobacco in it.

Hafizullah *nods.*

Zia   Crazy.

He shakes his head.

Hafizullah *shrugs and then licks the paper.*

Zia *winces slightly.*

A pause during which **Hafizullah** *finishes the joint. He approaches* **Zia**, *lights it for him and passes it over.*

Zia (*as he takes it*)   Thank you.

Hafizullah *nods in response and then goes and returns to his corner. Sits. Hums a Hindi pop tune briefly under his breath. Sighs. Rubs/scratches his head. Yawns.*

A pause during which **Zia** *inhales. Exhales.*

Zia   Rupert. Rupert.

Simon *turns round.*

Simon   . . . ?

Zia   Yeah, what is a. Cas . . . vac?

Simon   Airlift. Helicopter. Chinook.

Zia *nods.*

Zia   To the main . . . place?

Simon   Bastion, yeah.

Zia *nods.*

Zia   And how long till it like, gets here?

Simon   God knows.

Zia   Na, you must have some . . .

Simon   I really don't. Hours. Days. Millennia.

Zia   But is there no way you could like hurry it up or
something? Because basically my leg is really starting ta . . .

Simon   No, frankly.

Zia   Cos, I think . . . I really think . . .

Simon   It comes when it comes.

Zia *nods his head a little.*

He takes a drag. Exhales.

But, Rupert. Rupert, could you not . . . ?

Simon   Look, I don't know where you've got that from. But
my name isn't. Rupert.

Zia *nods.*

Zia (*referring to* **Gary**)   That's what he called you, though.

Simon   Did he?

Hafizullah Yes.

Simon Well, it's . . . it's not.

Zia OK.

He nods.

A pause, during which he inhales / exhales.

So why does he call you that?

Hafizullah Yes, why?

Simon Because.

He sighs.

Because it's a name used by . . .

Hafizullah What?

Simon . . . by, by people like the Corporal, to describe people . . .

Hafizullah Who are posh?

Simon What? *No.* Well, yes, in a way but . . . it's a name used . . . Jesus Christ, it's a *nickname* used to describe commissioned officers by lower and non-commissioned ranks. My name is Captain Mannock. And. That's. That.

Zia *nods.*

Hafizullah *nods.*

*A pause, during which **Zia** inhales / exhales.*

Zia Captain Man . . . Captain. Captain. I don't think you should let him back in here again.

Simon What?

Zia I don't.

Simon And why not?

Zia Cos he . . .

Simon . . . ?

Zia   Fucked up my leg.

Simon   . . . ?

Zia   While you were gone.

Simon   Did he?

Zia *nods.*

Zia   Even though you told him not to. Ask him. (*Referring to* **Hafizullah**.)

Simon (*to* **Hafizullah**)   . . . ?

Hafizullah *nods.*

Simon *nods.*

Simon   And are you . . . what did he . . . what did he do, exactly?

Zia   Jumped on it with his whole weight. Heard something break.

Simon   I'm sure it'll seem worse than . . .

Zia   No, I think there's some proper like long-term damage, I could be . . . really, I could be . . .

Simon   You'll . . . you'll be fine. When the medic's . . . when he's finished, with the others. He's really very good.

Zia   Not that good though, is he?

Simon   Well, I'm . . . that's . . . it wasn't his . . .

Zia   I mean, no . . . that's not what . . . not what I . . .

Simon   . . . his . . . his fault, or . . .

Zia   No no, I mean like, what if it's too late by then though, for me?

Simon   Well then. Then it's too late.

Zia   That's . . . but that's. Fucked up.

Simon   Yes. Yes it is. Welcome to Afghanistan.

Zia   But . . . are you . . . ? Are you gonna let him back in here though?

Pause.

Simon   He needs time to himself, anyway.

Zia   Right.

Simon   Yeah.

Zia   Thank you.

Simon   That's what he needs.

Zia *nods.*

Zia   Sounds like the right decision, I think.

Pause.

Simon   And – for the record – our medic. He couldn't have done any more to . . . Phipps was too far . . .

Zia *nods.*

Zia   Yeah, I can. Imagine.

Simon   Can you?

Zia *shrugs.*

Zia   Maybe.

Simon   Or – 'maybe' – you don't have to.

Zia   What?

Simon   I don't know.

Zia   What you saying?

Simon   Maybe you saw the state of him after you fired the fucking thing, Zia. I don't know.

Zia   But. No. I told you. (*Referring to* **Gary**.) Him. (*Referring to* **Hafizullah**.) Him.

Hafizullah   What?

Zia I told you.

Simon Yes.

Hafizullah . . . ?

Zia So what . . . what else you want from me?

Simon Maybe you're best off not pushing this.

Zia I ain't pushing, I'm asking you.

Simon I don't really see the difference.

Zia Look, I'm pretty fucking stoned here, mate, so I can't really get my head round what you . . . where you're . . . why . . . why you're thinking now all of sudden that I'm . . . that I was . . . ?

Simon All I am saying, is that I don't know. And, I've just watched one of my men bleed his last into this fuck-awful ground so please forgive me for maintaining a healthy level of fucking . . . scepticism.

Zia OK then, OK. I'll just shut up then, cos clearly I can't say nothing without . . . I'll be quiet now, yeah? Completely.

Simon I think it's a bit late for that.

Zia *nods.*

Zia Is it? So, if I talk I'm fucked and if I don't talk . . . I'm fucked?

Simon I don't give a . . . Listen to me. OK? I'm just here for the shade and to make sure that while we're waiting you don't have your head hacked off by one of the superb ANA recruits that we're meant to be fucking training here. (*To* **Hafizullah**.) Present company excepted.

Hafizullah *nods.*

Hafizullah Yes.

Simon So. Do, say what you like. Just. Don't expect me to believe a word of it or care if I hurt your obviously very delicate fucking Ali G fucking . . . terrorist . . . feelings. Alright? OK?

Zia *nods.*

Zia   ...

Simon   So is that OK with you then, Zia?

Zia *nods.*

Zia   ...

Simon   *Alhamdulillah.*

A long pause as **Zia** *inhales/exhales.*

Zia   Actually, though, you know what. It was me. I did it.

Pause.

Simon   What?

Hafizullah   ...?

Zia *nods.*

Zia   I can't lie to you no more. May as well . . . It was me.
I killed him. Your boy. (*Pause.*) And, and I want you to know,
I knew exactly what I was doing, when I done it. (*He nods.*)
Why. You should know that.

Simon   ...

Hafizullah   You.

Zia   Yeah. It's actually good to. Talk about it. Like. Get it off
my. Relief, almost. You know? Yeah. Breathe. (*Pause.*) All
started. This day. I was. I was walking round Whitechapel –
in London – and Osama Bin Laden he was outside this
Costcutter and he comes up to me as I go in and says, he
whispers to me: 'Bruv, say goodbye to Wanstead, you has got a
whole new mission now, my boy, goodness gracious me.'

He nods.

Simon   For fuck sake.

Zia   But, but I thought you didn't care what I say?

Simon   I don't.

Zia   No? Cos now you look like maybe you might.

Simon   No, I look like I've been on my feet since dawn fighting the . . . purest of the fucking pure.

Zia   OK then. OK. How about. This. I'm glad – I am – that your Geordie fucking *kuffar* fucking *ape*, I'm glad he's out there lying in his own fucking . . .

Simon   Zia.

Zia   Yeah, I am. You hear that?

Simon *takes a step towards him.*

Zia   But, but I thought you didn't care what I say? Maybe you was lying. Was you lying?

He smiles.

You were. Yeah. I caught you. See you.

Simon *shakes his head in disbelief at this, scoffs and moves towards the doorway.*

Zia   Sorry, am I wasting your time now? You got places to be?

Simon   No, I think you'd really rather I stay.

Zia   Yeah, I do.

He nods.

Simon *scoffs.*

Simon   You're a proper little fucker, aren't you?

Zia   No.

Simon   Yeah. Little weasel-type . . .

Zia   No no no, look at you, there. Stood there like. Like you know every thing to know about . . . Thinking you know all the . . . Thinking I'm like some . . . little . . . I always. Yeah, I always got people like you, looking at me like that, like I'm . . .

Simon   I wonder why.

Zia   No no, shut your *mouth*, yeah? Shut.

Simon   Even the way you speak is . . .

Zia   *Shut.*

Simon   I'm . . . no, I'm not gonna be . . .

Zia   No. You. You. *Shut.* I've had enough *white boys* talking today. They can listen now. Listen. This . . . I mean, this fucking . . . *country*. You. *People.*

He nods.

It's like living in *some* . . . I come to Lahore, just to get away from the the, the *noise of you*. Every . . . Like if it ain't some . . . some public-school blonde *bitch* trying to . . . teach me to . . . trying to make up for her own . . . *money* she got by somehow . . . then, then you got every little fucking *Paki boy* from here to Harrow, heading to the to the *masjid* with their, in their BMWs with their two, two, two fucking SIM cards, one for the *wife* they got *given* and then one, then, then *one* for the black girl they're fucking called Shanice or *Candice* or *whatever the fuck these people call themselves*, but then, then the *worst of the fucking* . . . You people. *All. You. People. GORA.* With your . . . your fat slut *women* to your fucking . . . *Surrey* . . . fucking . . . Richmond *fucking* . . . into *my fucking* . . . and always *talking* about your *trivial shit* like it's – hear you, hear you – like it's . . . you people, making all your *shit*, buying all the, all this *shit* you buy, watching all the *shit* you people, people like you people *make* while other people, my people, real people are . . . And then you get all like, all this like: 'Why are these people so angry? Why are these people so *fucking angry all the fucking time*?' *How?* (*Pause.*) How? How? How could I not be angry? *How the fuck could I not be angry, with that?* What I know about you people? Living with . . . You tell me that. *You fucking tell me that.* How?

Simon   . . .

Pause.

Zia (*softer, genuine*)   I mean it: how? Tell me – truthful – and I will . . . I will listen, to you. Now. Here. This. I will . . . I will. I will. (*Pause.*) What, you ain't got no answer for me?

Simon   . . .

Zia   Why, you deaf as well as Caucasian?

Simon   Zia.

Zia   Fucking. You know what? Give me the rucksack, bruv.
Give it. Now. I'll do it. I swear. As long as I don't have to *talk*
no more, *watch* any more fucking . . . Watch my . . . You.
Answer any more . . . You. Either that, yeah, or just shoot me.
Be the fuck. Done.

He nods.

I mean it. I do.

A long pause.

Simon   Feel better?

Zia (*genuine*)   No, no, I don't.

Simon   You know who you sound like?

Zia   Who?

Simon   My son.

Zia   Why? Is he a Muslim?

Simon   No. Worse than that. He's a goth.

Zia   Is it?

Simon   Yeah. And he's. Ungrateful. Self-important.
Incoherent. You've got it all.

Zia   Fuck you then.

Simon   Yeah, that's it. To a T.

Zia   Look, I don't care what you say.

Simon   And again, attaboy.

Zia   I'm . . . No. No. I'm just gonna wait for the fucking . . .
chairlift or airlift or . . . Seriously, I ain't, I ain't talking to you
no more.

Simon   Thank the good Lord for that.

He nods.

Zia *nods.*

A long pause.

Enter **Gary**.

Pause.

Gary   What's he on about now?

Hafizullah   I don't. Know.

Gary   No?

Hafizullah   Something.

Gary   Yeah?

Hafizullah *nods.*

Hafizullah   Yes.

Gary   Useful summary. Thank you, Paddy. (*Pause.*) Just been for a nice walk. Bit of fresh air. Does you the world. (*To* **Zia**.) You should try it.

Zia   Fuck all you.

Gary   Oh. Right. Get him to open up then, did we, sir?

Simon   Unfortunately.

Gary   Good stuff.

Simon   Ranting about . . . nothing.

Gary   Was he?

Simon   Yeah.

Gary *nods.*

Pause.

Said my goodbyes 'n that.

Simon   Yeah.

Gary   To him.

Simon   OK.

Gary   I did. All of it. (*Pause.*) Even asked him.

Simon   Asked him?

Gary   What I should do, sir.

Simon   OK.

Gary   But he didn't answer. Cos he's dead 'n that.

He shakes his head.

Pause.

Though I reckon sometimes you just know. Don't ya?

Pause.

Simon   I'm afraid you've lost me.

Gary   It's just fucking obvious, sometimes.

He takes out a pistol. Aims it at **Zia**.

Gary   Ain't it?

Zia *stiffens.*

Pause.

Gary   Reckon I'll get any virgins for this, sir?

Zia   . . .

Simon   Lance Corporal Harris. No.

Gary   Thought not.

Simon   Come on.

Gary   Keep hearing my name today. Like . . .

Simon   You can't . . .

Gary   Tinnitus. What? I can't what, sir?

Simon   You know.

Gary   No. You know what? I don't think I do.

Zia   Yeah, go on. Do it.

Gary   Yeah? You want me to?

Zia *nods.*

Zia   Please.

Gary   Alright.

Zia   Yeah.

In a rapid move, **Gary** *changes his grip on the pistol and hits* **Zia** *full across the face with the butt. The motion of this brings* **Gary** *back standing in front of, and facing,* **Hafizullah**. *Simultaneously,* **Simon** *moves towards* **Gary**, *but keeps a limited distance between them.* **Zia** *is slumped on the floor, his head a bloody mess.*

Gary   You see that, Paddy? You see it? Cos you know what? I've been thinking. Fuck your mum. Fuck her. I don't care no more. No one does. All you fucking . . . out here in the dirt like . . . Yeah, I don't think you wanna come any closer, sir.

Simon   Don't touch him again.

Gary   Na, he can take it.

Simon   I doubt that, very much.

Gary   Loves it. You heard him.

Simon   Move away.

Gary   *Na. (Pause.)* So what, doing the moves, so do they like teach a course at Sandhurst about how to deal with this kinda . . .

Simon   Put it down, or . . .

Gary   Like a fucking . . . role play or something?

Simon   I'm ordering you.

Gary *nods.*

Pause.

Gary   But I'd like to finish up, sir.

Simon   I'm not even sure he's still breathing.

Gary   He'll be right.

Simon   I don't think he will. Look at him.

Gary   Na na, you look, sir. His chest. Moving 'n that. See him?

Pause.

Simon   You can walk away from this. If you put it down.

Gary   But . . . ? But how would we fucking explain all this, sir?

Simon   You can. If you listen to me.

Gary   I'm not sure I want to, though.

Simon   I think you do.

Gary   Well . . . then. Then you're even more of a cunt than I thought you was, sir. Like. Since we got here. We've been sitting around, waiting for a fight. Well, now I got one. (*Pause.*) How many people you killed, sir?

Simon   Enough.

Gary   Yeah, well, I'm pretty much the only one who didn't slot anyone the last few days and this'll be my first, so who are you to fucking . . .

Simon   I'm your commanding officer.

Gary   Oh yeah. Forgot. (*Pause.*) You alright there, Paddy? Surprised you're not piping up. Asking me to walk away, chill the fuck out, bruv.

Hafizullah   . . .

Gary   And, and, Paddy ain't his real name, sir. Na. Just call him that.

Simon   OK.

Gary You know like, luck of the Irish? He's a lucky fucker so . . . always fucking off his . . . but he still manages to . . . somehow . . .

Simon Great.

Gary Yeah, well, I thought it was really fucking funny actually, sir.

Hafizullah Hafizullah. My name.

Simon *nods.*

Simon OK.

Gary Yeah, that's it.

Simon . . .

Gary But I prefer Paddy, cos I can say it.

Hafizullah Hafizullah.

Gary Yeah.

Simon Give me the gun.

Hafizullah Yes.

Gary What was your school like, sir?

Simon What?

Gary What was your school like?

Pause.

Simon Big. Old.

Gary Yeah. Mine was small. And shit. (*Referring to* **Zia**.) Full of cunts like him. Bet yours weren't.

Simon No, mine was full of cunts like me.

Gary Exactly.

Simon And I rather enjoyed it.

Gary *nods.*

Gary   Yeah. Mine was like a fucking . . . (*Pause.*) I ain't even got the words for it, to be honest, sir. But that's to be expected, ain't it?

Simon *shrugs.*

Simon   I don't know.

Gary   Yeah, way it is. Like. My dad. He's an old fucker. He was in Aden. Doing shit like this. For cunts like you. And my grandad. India. And it's. Thick cunts, led by posh cunts, hitting brown cunts. Way it is. Even now.

Simon   I think it's a little bit more complicated than that.

Gary   Is it? Where is it? So. So this shit. This. This is my birthright.

He taps his chest.

Pause.

Yeah, yeah, no, you're right. He has stopped breathing. Look at him. All. Still. (*Pause.*) Oh no. There he is.

Simon   Move away.

Gary   Up a little bit. Down. (*Pause.*) You're not really listening to me, are ya, sir?

Simon   Every word.

Gary   Are ya?

Simon *nods.*

Simon   And you know what's happening. You know what you're doing here.

Gary   Do I?

Simon   To this man.

Gary   Cunt.

Simon   What you've done to him. What this will mean. What you're going to do. (*Pause.*) And yeah, I've done a few courses. Yes, I understand what you feel. And yes, I think we should end this. Properly.

Gary   What, like, do him in?

Pause.

Simon   We've killed enough people today. The right people.

Gary   So we're done murdering, now it's my turn? Sir.

Simon   This isn't . . .

Gary   Typical.

Simon   He's a boy.

Gary   I thought you said he was a man.

Simon   He is, what he is. And you're not going to kill him.

Gary   Sir. (*Pause.*) Sir.

Simon   Lance Corporal. You're mine. You are. And I'm not going to let you do this. Give me the fucking thing, now.

He moves forward, reaches out with his hand, palm downwards.

A very long pause.

Gary *hands over the gun.*

Simon   Thank you.

Gary   . . .

Simon   It's loaded?

Gary *nods.*

Gary   Yeah, it's a gun.

Simon *nods. Smiles a little.*

Simon   Yeah.

Gary   And I should a' fucking used it. Shouldn't I, Paddy?

Hafizullah   Fuck you.

Hafizullah *nods.*

Gary   Rowdy.

Hafizullah   Please. You. All of this. Please.

Gary *considers* **Hafizullah**.

Gary   Paddy's having a paddy, sir.

Hafizullah   Hafizullah.

Gary   Whatever.

Hafizullah   My name.

Gary   Yeah, OK.

Hafizullah   My name.

A pause before they start to hear the Chinook beginning to approach/descend.

Gary   Fuck.

Simon   *God.*

They listen.

Gary   So what do we do now, sir?

The noise of the helicopter starts to increase. Sand/dust begins to blow in through the door.

What the fuck do we do?

The noise increases. More sand/dust. First wafts, then clouds of it.

Simon   . . .

The noise is immense.

Hafizullah *grabs his head, trying to push out the sound.*

Blackout.

Methuen Drama Student Editions

Jean Anouilh *Antigone* • John Arden *Serjeant Musgrave's Dance*
Alan Ayckbourn *Confusions* • Aphra Behn *The Rover* • Edward Bond
Lear • *Saved* • Bertolt Brecht *The Caucasian Chalk Circle* • *Fear and
Misery in the Third Reich* • *The Good Person of Szechwan* • *Life of Galileo* •
Mother Courage and her Children • *The Resistible Rise of Arturo Ui* • *The
Threepenny Opera* • Anton Chekhov *The Cherry Orchard* • *The Seagull* •
Three Sisters • *Uncle Vanya* • Caryl Churchill *Serious Money* • *Top Girls*
• Shelagh Delaney *A Taste of Honey* • Euripides *Elektra* • *Medea* •
Dario Fo *Accidental Death of an Anarchist* • Michael Frayn *Copenhagen*
• John Galsworthy *Strife* • Nikolai Gogol *The Government Inspector* •
Robert Holman *Across Oka* • Henrik Ibsen *A Doll's House* • *Ghosts* •
Hedda Gabler • Charlotte Keatley *My Mother Said I Never Should* •
Bernard Kops *Dreams of Anne Frank* • Federico García Lorca *Blood
Wedding* • *Doña Rosita the Spinster* (bilingual edition) • *The House of
Bernarda Alba* • (bilingual edition) • *Yerma* (bilingual edition) • David
Mamet *Glengarry Glen Ross* • *Oleanna* • Patrick Marber *Closer* • John
Marston *Malcontent* • Martin McDonagh *The Lieutenant of Inishmore* •
Joe Orton *Loot* • Luigi Pirandello *Six Characters in Search of an Author*
• Mark Ravenhill *Shopping and F***ing* • Willy Russell *Blood Brothers*
• *Educating Rita* • Sophocles *Antigone* • *Oedipus the King* • Wole
Soyinka *Death and the King's Horseman* • Shelagh Stephenson *The
Memory of Water* • August Strindberg *Miss Julie* • J. M. Synge *The
Playboy of the Western World* • Theatre Workshop *Oh What a Lovely
War* Timberlake Wertenbaker *Our Country's Good* • Arnold Wesker
The Merchant • Oscar Wilde *The Importance of Being Earnest* •
Tennessee Williams *A Streetcar Named Desire* • *The Glass Menagerie*

Methuen Drama Contemporary Dramatists

include

John Arden (two volumes)
Arden & D'Arcy
Peter Barnes (three volumes)
Sebastian Barry
Dermot Bolger
Edward Bond (eight volumes)
Howard Brenton
 (two volumes)
Richard Cameron
Jim Cartwright
Caryl Churchill (two volumes)
Sarah Daniels (two volumes)
Nick Darke
David Edgar (three volumes)
David Eldridge
Ben Elton
Dario Fo (two volumes)
Michael Frayn (three volumes)
David Greig
John Godber (four volumes)
Paul Godfrey
John Guare
Lee Hall (two volumes)
Peter Handke
Jonathan Harvey
 (two volumes)
Declan Hughes
Terry Johnson (three volumes)
Sarah Kane
Barrie Keeffe
Bernard-Marie Koltès
 (two volumes)
Franz Xaver Kroetz
David Lan
Bryony Lavery
Deborah Levy
Doug Lucie

David Mamet (four volumes)
Martin McDonagh
Duncan McLean
Anthony Minghella
 (two volumes)
Tom Murphy (six volumes)
Phyllis Nagy
Anthony Neilsen (two volumes)
Philip Osment
Gary Owen
Louise Page
Stewart Parker (two volumes)
Joe Penhall (two volumes)
Stephen Poliakoff
 (three volumes)
David Rabe (two volumes)
Mark Ravenhill (two volumes)
Christina Reid
Philip Ridley
Willy Russell
Eric-Emmanuel Schmitt
Ntozake Shange
Sam Shepard (two volumes)
Wole Soyinka (two volumes)
Simon Stephens (two volumes)
Shelagh Stephenson
David Storey (three volumes)
Sue Townsend
Judy Upton
Michel Vinaver
 (two volumes)
Arnold Wesker (two volumes)
Michael Wilcox
Roy Williams (three volumes)
Snoo Wilson (two volumes)
David Wood (two volumes)
Victoria Wood